Teaching
the Bahá'í Faith

Teaching
the Bahá'í Faith

Compilations and a Statement Prepared by the Research
Department of the Universal House of Justice

Bahá'í Publications Australia

© Bahá'í Publications Australia
P.O. Box 285
Mona Vale NSW 2103
Phone: (61) 2 913 1554
    Fax: (61) 2 970 6710

Printed 1995

ISBN 0 909991 68 5

Cover illustration by Mariya Daliri Beale

Printed by Australian Print Group, Maryborough, Victoria, Australia

Table of Contents

PROMOTING ENTRY BY TROOPS

A Statement Prepared by the Research Department of the Universal
House of Justice
October 1993

PROMOTING ENTRY BY TROOPS

A Statement Prepared by the Research Department of the Universal
House of Justice
October 1993

Shoghi Effendi's vision of the organic unfoldment of the Faith shapes our
perception of the glorious future possibilities in the teaching field. In a letter
addressed to the American believers in 1953 where he points to the need for
deploying pioneers, the beloved Guardian states that "a steady flow of
reinforcements" will

> presage and hasten the advent of the day which, as prophesied by
> 'Abdu'l-Bahá, will witness the entry by troops of peoples of divers
> nations and races into the Bahá'í world — a day which, viewed in
> its proper perspective, will be the prelude to that long-awaited hour
> when mass conversion on the part of these same nations and races,
> and as a direct result of a chain of events, momentous and possibly
> catastrophic in nature ..., will suddenly revolutionize the fortunes of
> the Faith, derange the equilibrium of the world, and reinforce a
> thousandfold the numerical strength as well as the material power
> and the spiritual authority of the Faith of Bahá'u'lláh.[1]

Writing in its 1990 Riḍván message, the Universal House of Justice links
the "increasing instances of entry by troops" in different parts of the world to
the developmental stages described by Shoghi Effendi. It also fixes our place
in this historical process and challenges the believers to action. The House of
Justice attests:

> We have every encouragement to believe that large-scale enrolments
> will expand, involving village after village, town after town, from
> one country to another. However, it is not for us to wait passively for
> the ultimate fulfilment of Shoghi Effendi's vision. We few, placing
> our whole trust in the providence of God and regarding as a divine
> privilege the challenges which face us, must proceed to victory with
> the plans in hand.[2]

To assist the friends in refining their understanding of the processes
associated with entry by troops and in responding to the challenge posed by

the House of Justice we attach a compilation of extracts from letters written by or on behalf of Shoghi Effendi and the Universal House of Justice, and we offer the following comments aimed at exploring and highlighting some of the themes drawn from the compilation. In sections 1 and 2 of this statement, we describe a number of general features of the growth process and call attention to factors that contribute to the expansion of the Faith, while, in section 3, we focus on specific activities that can be undertaken to promote and sustain the process of entry by troops.

1. Some Characteristics of Growth

Before considering the subject of entry by troops we begin by examining a number of general features associated with the processes by which the Bahá'í Faith grows.

1.1 Organic Growth

The growth of the Faith proceeds in an organic, evolutionary manner.[3] Its rate of growth is, therefore, not necessarily uniform,[4] rather, it advances "in vast surges, precipitated by the alternation of crisis and victory".[5] Shoghi Effendi has also stated that the spread of the Faith all over the world will be accompanied by an acceleration of its rate of growth.[6]

For the present, the Faith is not growing at the same rate throughout the world. The Universal House of Justice has observed that there is an "eager receptivity" to the Faith in many lands,[7] and that certain segments of the population may, initially, tend to be more responsive than others to the Cause.[8] In those areas where the receptivity is just beginning to dawn, the House of Justice counsels the believers to have confidence that "the time is coming when the number of their fellow-countrymen who accept the Faith will suddenly increase".[9]

With regard to the immediate future, the Universal House of Justice affirms that the rate of growth is destined to accelerate. It states that "the stage is set for universal, rapid and massive growth of the Cause",[10] and it envisages that all national communities will reap the harvest of entry by troops.[11]

1.2 Dynamic of Crisis and Victory

The dynamic interplay of the processes of crisis and victory characterizes the development of the Faith.[12] Shoghi Effendi affirms that "the record of its tumultuous history" demonstrates

the supreme truth that with every fresh outbreak of hostility to the Faith, whether from within or from without, a corresponding measure of outpouring grace, sustaining its defenders and confounding its adversaries, has been providentially released, communicating a fresh impulse to the onward march of the Faith, while this impetus, in its turn, would, through its manifestations, provoke fresh hostility in quarters heretofore unaware of its challenging implications...[13]

The Universal House of Justice, likewise, allies the continuing emergence of the Faith from obscurity and the maturation of the functioning of the administrative institutions with the community's response to the recent wave of persecutions in Iran[14] and it foreshadows that "the present victories will lead to active opposition".[15]

1.3 Impact of Social Decline

Shoghi Effendi calls attention to the purifying influence of suffering and tribulation, associated with the process of social decline, on the expansion of the Faith.[16] And, in a letter written on his behalf, the Guardian notes that "after mankind has suffered ... people will enter the Cause of God in troops".[17]

The Universal House of Justice graphically depicts the impact of the declining process on humanity, relates it to mankind's spiritual search[18] and underlines the pressing responsibility of the Bahá'ís, both to increase the tempo of their teaching activities,[19] "lest opportunity be lost in the swiftly changing moods of a frenetic world",[20] and to create the kind of community that offers such a distinctive pattern of life that it will "rekindle hope among the increasingly disillusioned members of society".[21]

1.4 Emergence from Obscurity

The progress of the Faith is hastened by the opportunities afforded by its emergence from obscurity. The Universal House of Justice refers to "the emergence of a new paradigm of opportunity for further growth and consolidation of our world-wide community",[22] and it underlines the urgent challenge facing the Bahá'í community to meet the needs of the possibilities that arise as the Lesser Peace approaches.[23]

2. Factors Contributing to Growth

By way of introduction, it is important to observe that the beloved Guardian, in a letter dated 18 February 1932 written on his behalf, underscores the fact that a mere increase in the number of believers does not necessarily connote progress of the Cause. He states:

> It is not sufficient to number the souls that embrace the Cause to know the progress that it is making. The more important consequences of your activities are the spirit that is diffused into the life of the community, and the extent to which the teachings we proclaim become part of the consciousness and belief of the people that hear them. For it is only when the spirit has thoroughly permeated the world that the people will begin to enter the Faith in large numbers.[24]

Likewise, in the 1989 Ridván message, the Universal House of Justice affirms:

> It is not enough to proclaim the Bahá'í message, essential as that is. It is not enough to expand the rolls of Bahá'í membership, vital as that is. Souls must be transformed, communities thereby consolidated, new models of life thus attained. Transformation is the essential purpose of the Cause of Bahá'u'lláh, but it lies in the will and effort of the individual to achieve it in obedience to the Covenant.[25]

From a study of the letters of Shoghi Effendi and the Universal House of Justice it is possible to identify several factors that contribute to the large-scale growth of the Faith. These factors interact with and reinforce each other and, when they operate in concert, they provide the basis for the creation of a growth-producing milieu — a Bahá'í community whose members are dedicated to refining their understanding of the nature of teaching and to learning how to work together in ways that will both accelerate and sustain the processes of expansion and consolidation. Included among these interactive factors are the following.

2.1 Commitment to Spiritual Transformation

The crucial link between individual transformation and the gradual maturation of the functioning of the Bahá'í community and the growth of the Faith is a familiar theme in the letters of Shoghi Effendi and the Universal House of Justice. Fostering such transformation in personal and family life, in the functioning of communities and Assemblies is the responsibility of individuals[26] and Bahá'í institutions, alike.[27] As Shoghi Effendi explains:

> When the true spirit of teaching, which calls for complete dedication, consecration to the noble mission, and living the life, is fulfilled, not only by the individuals, but by the Assemblies also, then the Faith will grow by leaps and bounds.[28]

2.2 Love and Unity

Love and unity among the believers[29] and love of the friends for the Faith and its institutions[30] are fundamental to attracting large numbers of people to the Cause. The beloved Guardian describes unity and love among the friends as "the spirit which must animate their Community life",[31] and he spells out their practical implications in relation to the planning and implementation of the teaching work. In a letter written on his behalf, he guides the believers as follows:

> Let them put more effort into perfecting their purely Bahá'í relationships, become more united, more spiritually educated, more skilled in fulfilling their administrative tasks, as a preparation to teaching and welcoming larger numbers of new believers.[32]

The Universal House of Justice calls attention to another important aspect of this subject. It cautions against the polarization of views about teaching methods and approaches, and offers the following advice to the believers:

> In this, as in all aspects of the work of the Cause, the solution lies in the friends' being patient and forbearing towards those whose shortcomings distress them, and in endeavouring, through the Assemblies' consultation, to draw closer to a proper balance while maintaining the momentum of the work and canalizing the enthusiasm of the believers.[33]

2.3 Universal Participation

Universal participation and persistent efforts by the friends to teach the Cause, to apply its principles, and to furthur the development of its institutions are not only "indispensable to developing the human resources necessary to the progress of the Cause"[34] but they also enhance success in teaching.[35]

2.4 Balance Between Expansion and Consolidation

The Universal House of Justice refers to expansion and consolidation as "twin processes that must go hand in hand".[36] It states that they are "inseparable processes",[37] and that they represent "the primary objectives of teaching".[38] Stressing the relationship between consolidation and teaching, the House of Justice in a letter written on its behalf stated:

> Proper consolidation is essential to the preservation of the spiritual health of the community, to the protection of its interests, to the upholding of its good name, and ultimately to the continuation of the work of expansion itself.[39]

2.5 Bahá'í Community as a Model

The Bahá'í community and the Administrative Order must continue to be developed and presented to the world as a viable model and an alternative means of social organization. This is an ongoing process. Shoghi Effendi, in a letter written on his behalf, attests that:

> Until the public sees in the Bahá'í Community a true pattern, in action, of something better than it already has, it will not respond to the Faith in large numbers.[40]

In like manner, the Universal House of Justice calls attention to the distinctiveness of the Bahá'í community and states that, as the contrast between the community and the world at large increases, it "must eventually attract the disillusioned masses and cause them to enter the haven of the Covenant of Bahá'u'lláh".[41] Further, the House of Justice notes that there is increasing concern about the affairs of mankind and the inability of the old order to solve critical social problems. Since the Bahá'í Administrative Order is designed to be a pattern for future society, there is a pressing need to demonstrate "the potentialities inherent in the administrative system" and to provide, thereby, "a signal of hope to those who despair".[42]

Given the close relationships between elements of growth described above and their interactive nature, it is suggested that while each factor contributes to the expansion process, no one factor, by itself, would appear to be sufficient to produce and sustain large-scale enrolments. To concentrate on one to the exclusion of the others may well distort the teaching process and retard the long-term growth and expansion of the Bahá'í community. Further, Shoghi Effendi affirms that engagement in the teaching work reinforces the development of the very factors that contribute to the growth of the Faith. In a letter written on his behalf, he states:

> Action inspired by confidence in the ultimate triumph of the Faith is, indeed, essential to the gradual and complete materialization of your hopes for the extension and consolidation of the Movement in your country.[43]

The Guardian also calls attention to the danger inherent in the friends' waiting until they are "<u>fully</u> qualified to do any particular task",[44] and he stresses the relationship between individual effort and divine assistance, observing that:

> God will ... assist us if we do our share and sacrifice in the path of the progress of His Faith. We have to feel the responsibility laid upon our shoulders, arise to carry it out, and then expect divine grace to be showered upon us.[45]

3. Promoting Entry by Troops

From a study of the attached compilation, it is apparent that there are a number of specific activities that contribute directly to the process of entry by troops.

3.1 Strengthening of Spiritual Assemblies

Shoghi Effendi stresses the importance of the "instrumentality" of the Administrative Order in "vividly" and "systematically" bringing the healing Message of Bahá'u'lláh "to the attention of the masses".[46] He emphasizes the relationship between the development of the institutions and "the acceleration in the vital process of individual conversion", affirming that this latter is the reason for which "the entire machinery of the Administrative Order has been primarily and so laboriously erected".[47] Likewise, the Universal House of

Justice directly links the strengthening and development of Local Spiritual Assemblies with the capacity of the Faith to deal with entry by troops.[48] The nature of this relationship is explained by the House of Justice in the 1993 Riḍván message. It refers to "the mutuality of teaching and administration" and the fact that "each reinforces the other".[49]

The House of Justice indicates that there is an imperative need for Bahá'í institutions to

> improve their performance, through a closer identification with the fundamental verities of the Faith, through greater conformity to the spirit and form of Bahá'í administration and through a keener reliance on the beneficial effects of proper consultation, so that the communities they guide will reflect a pattern of life that will offer hope to the disillusioned members of society.[50]

To this end, the Universal House of Justice stresses the importance of training the friends, including those in mass teaching areas,[51] to increase their understanding of and participation in the administrative work of the Cause. It notes that the "proper functioning" of the Spiritual Assemblies

> depends largely on the efforts of their members to familiarize themselves with their duties and to adhere scrupulously to principle in their personal behaviour and in the conduct of their official responsibilities.

It calls attention to the importance of the Assembly members'

> resolve to remove all traces of estrangement and sectarian tendencies from their midst, their ability to win the affection and support of the friends under their care and to involve as many individuals as possible in the work of the Cause.

And it affirms that the outcome of such dedicated effort on the part of the members of the institutions will result in "a pattern of life" that will not only be "a credit to the Faith" but will also serve to attract the "increasingly disillusioned members of society".[52]

3.2 Efficient Administration and Prompt Consolidation

While the way in which the teaching work is organized is a matter for each National Spiritual Assembly to determine, the Universal House of Justice stresses the need for "an efficient teaching structure" to ensure that "the tasks are carried out with dispatch and in accordance with the administrative principles of our Faith".[53] It further states that the work of consolidation, which is "an essential and inseparable element of teaching",[54] must be "prompt, thorough and continuing".[55] Such an integrated approach to the expansion of the Cause not only increases the human and financial resources of the Bahá'í community,[56] it also helps to avoid such problems as the inoculation" of believers against the Faith, resulting from a combination of inadequate teaching and careless consolidation.[57]

3.3 Strategic, Flexible Teaching Plans

The Universal House of Justice calls upon each National Spiritual Assembly to "balance its resources and harmonize its efforts" to ensure that the Faith is taught to "all sections of society".[58] It advises the Assemblies to be strategic and systematic, to tailor their teaching plans to meet the needs of particular social and cultural groups,[59] since "different cultures and types of people require different methods of approach",[60] and it states that the aim of all Bahá'í institutions and Bahá'í teachers is "to advance continually to new areas and strata of society".[61]

The House of Justice draws attention to the importance of flexibility and balance in the formulation and implementation of teaching plans. The believers are encouraged to be open to new methods,[62] to use a variety of approaches,[63] and "not blindly insist upon doing the same thing everywhere".[64] The Universal House of Justice indicates that the Bahá'í community

> must become more adept at accommodating a wide range of actions without losing concentration on the primary objectives of teaching, namely, expansion and consolidation.

And to this end, it stresses the need for

> a unity in diversity of actions ..., a condition in which different individuals will concentrate on different activities, appreciating the salutary effect of the aggregate on the growth and development of

the Faith, because each person cannot do everything and all persons cannot do the same thing.[65]

The importance of the adoption by the believers of a strategic and flexible approach to the work of the Cause is linked by the Universal House of Justice both to the growing maturity of the Bahá'í community and to its expansion.[66]

3.4 Reaching People of Capacity

Writing to the National Spiritual Assemblies, the Universal House of Justice directed that the Faith must be carried "to every stratum of human society and every walk of life". It further stated that "all must be brought consciously within the teaching plans of the Bahá'í Community."[67]

Given the need to increase and develop the human resources of the Faith, the Universal House of Justice calls upon the believers to address special efforts to attracting people of capacity to the Cause.[68] It describes the enrolment of people of capacity as "an indispensable aspect of teaching the masses", and cautions that failure to achieve this end will result in the Faith's not being able "adequately to meet the challenges being thrust upon it". Concerning the membership of the Bahá'í community and the priorities for the teaching work, the House of Justice states:

> Its membership, regardless of ethnic variety, needs now to embrace increasing numbers of people of capacity, including persons of accomplishment and prominence in the various fields of human endeavour. Enrolling significant numbers of such persons is an indispensable aspect of teaching the masses, an aspect which cannot any longer be neglected and which must be consciously and deliberately incorporated into our teaching work, so as to broaden its base and accelerate the process of entry by troops.[69]

3.5 Relating the Faith to Contemporary Social and Humanitarian Issues

In the Riḍván 1988 message, the Universal House of Justice listed the individual believer's "constant endeavour" to relate the Teachings of the Faith to "current issues" as one of the measures which contribute to "success in teaching".[70] The House of Justice also notes that the "Order brought by Bahá'u'lláh is intended to guide the progress and resolve the problems of society", and that the Bahá'í community is "clearly in the vanguard of the constructive forces at work on the planet". It calls attention to the need to develop and perfect the Bahá'í administrative system as a means of demonstrating the efficacy of this system to minister to the crying needs of humanity, and to offer it as a viable alternative" to the defective crumbling old world order.[71]

3.6 Goal-Directed Behaviour

Individual believers, Local and National Spiritual Assemblies are called upon to collaborate and persist in their efforts to achieve the goals of the teaching plans. The Universal House of Justice states:

> The teaching work, both that organized by institutions of the Faith and that which is the fruit of individual initiative, must be actively carried forward so that there will be growing numbers of believers, leading more countries to the stage of entry by troops and ultimately to mass conversion.[72]

The urgency of this undertaking is emphasized by the House of Justice, as follows:

> A massive expansion of the Bahá'í community must be achieved far beyond all past records. The task of spreading the Message to the generality of mankind in villages, towns and cities must be rapidly extended. The need for this is critical...[73]

In addition, the Universal House of Justice calls attention to the quality of the teaching enterprise, advising that "the effort of the Bahá'ís should be to teach not only as intensively as possible but also as well as possible".[74]

The ultimate responsibility of the individual believer for the implementation of the teaching work is underlined by the House of Justice. It states:

> Every individual believer — man, woman, youth and child — is summoned to this field of action; for it is on the initiative, the resolute will of the individual to teach and to serve, that the success of the entire community depends.[75]

And it affirms that:

The key to the conversion of people to the Faith is the action of the individual Bahá'í conveying the spark of faith to individual seekers, answering their questions and deepening their understanding of the teachings.[76]

4. Concluding Remarks

The extracts contained in the compilation "Promoting Entry by Troops" serve to highlight a number of general principles relating to the nature of growth and its acceleration and to the attraction of large numbers of people to the Bahá'í Faith. In addition, the extracts suggest specific activities that can be undertaken, by individuals and institutions, to increase the tempo of growth and to sustain large-scale expansion of the Cause.

It is evident that forces without and within the Cause are shaping the destiny of humanity. The Universal House of Justice calls attention to the operation of two great processes that are at work in the world. The first process is

the great Plan of God, tumultuous in its progress, working through mankind as a whole, tearing down barriers to world unity and forging humankind into a unified body in the fires of suffering and experience. This process will produce, in God's due time, the Lesser Peace, the political unification of the world. Mankind at that time can be likened to a body that is unified but without life. The second process, the task of breathing life into this unified body — of creating true unity and spirituality culminating in the Most Great Peace — is that of the Bahá'ís, who are labouring consciously, with detailed instructions and continuing divine guidance, to erect the fabric of the Kingdom of God on earth, into which they call their fellow-men, thus conferring upon them eternal life.[77]

The challenge to the believers is to devote all their energies to this vital task, spurred on by the realization that "there is no one else to do it",[78] and sustained by their desire to fulfil the longing expressed by the beloved Guardian in the earliest days of his ministry:

And now as I look into the future, I hope to see the friends at all times, in every land, and of every shade of thought and character, voluntarily and joyously rallying round their local and in particular their national centres of activity, upholding and promoting their interests with complete unanimity and contentment, with perfect understanding, genuine enthusiasm, and sustained vigour. This indeed is the one joy and yearning of my life, for it is the fountain-head from which all future blessings will flow, the broad foundation upon which the security of the Divine Edifice must ultimately rest. May we not hope that now at last the dawn of a brighter day is breaking upon our beloved Cause?[79]

REFERENCES

Note: The numbers in brackets following each reference correspond to the numbering of the extracts in the attached compilation.

1.   Letter dated 25 June 1953 written by Shoghi Effendi, published in "Citadel of Faith: Messages to America 1947-1957" (Wilmette: Bahá'í Publishing Trust, 1980), p. 117 [18]*

2.   Riḍván 1990 message written by the Universal House of Justice to the Bahá'ís of the world [45]

3.   See extract [2]

4.   See extract [33]

5.   Letter dated 31 August 1987 written by the Universal House of Justice to the Bahá'ís of the world [39]

6.   Letter dated 30 June 1952 written on behalf of Shoghi Effendi to a National Spiritual Assembly [17]

7.   Naw-Rúz 1979 message written by the Universal House of Justice to the Bahá'ís of the world [32]; see also extracts [34] and [44]

8.   See extract [41]

9.   Letter dated 12 September 1991 written on behalf of the Universal House of Justice to a National Spiritual Assembly [46]

---

*   Published version gives date as 18 July 1953.

10. Riḍván 1987 message written by the Universal House of Justice to the Bahá'ís of the world **[38]**

11. See extract **[44]**

12. See extract **[21]**

13. Postcript in the handwriting of Shoghi Effendi appended to a letter dated 12 August 1941 written on his behalf, cf. "Messages to America: Selected Letters and Cablegrams Addressed to the Bahá'ís of North America, 1932-1946" (Wilmette: Bahá'í Publishing Committee, 1947), p. 51 **[6]**

14. See extract **[40]**

15. Message dated 27 December 1985 written by the Universal House of Justice to the Conference of the Continental Boards of Counsellors **[36]**

16. See extracts **[4]** and **[13]**

17. Letter dated 5 October 1953 written on behalf of Shoghi Effendi to an individual believer **[19]**

18. See extract **[24]**

19. See extract **[38]**

20. Riḍván 1988 message written by the Universal House of Justice to the Bahá'ís of the world **[40]**

21. Riḍván 1993 message written by the Universal House of Justice to the Bahá'ís of the world **[48]**

22. Riḍván 1988 message written by the Universal House of Justice to the Bahá'ís of the world **[40]**

23. See extracts **[35]**, **[44]**, and **[47]**

24. Letter dated 18 February 1932 written on behalf of Shoghi Effendi to an individual believer **[2]**

25. Riḍván 1989 message written by the Universal House of Justice to the Bahá'ís of the world **[44]**

26. See extracts **[16]** and **[40]**

27. See extract **[25]**

28. Letter dated 19 March 1954 written on behalf of Shoghi Effendi to a Local Spiritual Assembly **[20]**

29. See extract **[8]**

30. See extract **[15]**

31. Letter dated 13 March 1944 written on behalf of Shoghi Effendi to a Bahá'í winter school session **[9]**; see also extract **[11]**

32. Letter dated 25 March 1949 written on behalf of Shoghi Effendi to an individual believer **[14]**

33. Letter dated 30 June 1993 written on behalf of the Universal House of Justice to an individual believer **[49]**

34. Riḍván 1993 message written by the Universal House of Justice to the Bahá'ís of the world **[48]**

35. See extract **[40]**

36. Letter dated 13 July 1964 written by the Universal House of Justice to all National Spiritual Assemblies, cf. "Wellspring of Guidance: Messages 1963-1968" (Wilmette: Bahá'í Publishing Trust, 1976), pp. 31-33 **[23]**

37. Letter dated 2 February 1966 written by the Universal House of Justice to all National Spiritual Assemblies engaged in mass teaching work **[25]**

38. Riḍván 1990 message written by the Universal House of Justice to the Bahá'ís of the world **[45]**

39. Letter dated 17 April 1981 written by the Universal House of Justice to all National Spiritual Assemblies **[35]**

40. Letter dated 13 March 1944 written on behalf of Shoghi Effendi to an individual believer **[10]**

41. Message dated August 1968 written by the Universal House of Justice to the Palermo Conference, cf. "Messages from the Universal House of Justice, 1968-1973" (Wilmette: Bahá'í Publishing Trust, 1976), p. 12 **[28]**

42. Riḍván 1990 message written by the Universal House of Justice to the Bahá'ís of the world **[45]**

43. Letter dated 11 May 1934 written on behalf of Shoghi Effendi to an individual believer **[5]**

44. Letter dated 4 May 1942 written on behalf of Shoghi Effendi to an individual believer **[7]**

45. Letter dated 20 December 1932 written on behalf of Shoghi Effendi to a National Spiritual Assembly **[3]**

46. Postcript in the handwriting of Shoghi Effendi appended to a letter dated 29 March 1945 written on his behalf to a National Spiritual Assembly **[12]**

47. Postcript in the handwriting of Shoghi Effendi appended to a letter dated 12 August 1957 written on his behalf to a National Spiritual Assembly **[22]**

48. See extract **[30]**

49. Riḍván 1993 message written by the Universal House of Justice to the Bahá'ís of the world **[48]**

50. Riḍván 1990 message written by the Universal House of Justice to the Bahá'ís of the world **[45]**

51. See extract **[32]**

52. Riḍván 1993 message written by the Universal House of Justice to the Bahá'ís of the world **[48]**

53. Letter dated 2 February 1966 written by the Universal House of Justice to all National Spiritual Assemblies engaged in mass teaching work **[25]**

54. Letter dated 16 April 1981 written on behalf of the Universal House of Justice to all Continental Pioneer Committees **[34]**

55. Naw-Rúz 1979 message written by the Universal House of Justice to the Bahá'ís of the world **[32]**

56. See extract **[36]**

57. See extract **[34]**

58. Letter dated 13 July 1964 written by the Universal House of Justice to all National Spiritual Assemblies, cf. "Wellspring of Guidance", pp. 31-33 **[23]**

59. See extract **[26]**

60. Letter dated 11 August 1988 written on behalf of the Universal House of Justice to an individual believer **[41]**

61.   Letter dated 25 May 1975 written by the Universal House of Justice to all National Spiritual Assemblies **[31]**

62.   See extract **[29]**

63.   See extract **[43]**

64.   Letter dated 13 November 1986 written on behalf of the Universal House of Justice to a National Spiritual Assembly **[37]**

65.   Riḍván 1990 message written by the Universal House of Justice to the Bahá'ís of the world **[45]**

66.   See extract **[37]**

67.   Letter dated 31 October 1967 written by the Universal House of Justice to all National Spiritual Assemblies, cf. "Wellspring of Guidance", pp. 124-25 **[26]**

68.   See extract **[48]**

69.   Riḍván 1990 message written by the Universal House of Justice to the Bahá'ís of the world **[45]**

70.   Riḍván 1988 message written by the Universal House of Justice to the Bahá'ís of the world **[40]**

71.   Riḍván 1990 message written by the Universal House of Justice to the Bahá'ís of the world **[45]**

72.   Naw-Rúz 1979 message written by the Universal House of Justice to the Bahá'ís of the world **[32]**

73.   Riḍván 1993 message written by the Universal House of Justice to the Bahá'ís of the world **[48]**

74.   Letter dated 1 November 1988 written on behalf of the Universal House of Justice to a National Spiritual Assembly **[42]**

75.   Riḍván 1988 message written by the Universal House of Justice to the Bahá'ís of the world **[40]**

76.   Letter dated 9 February 1989 written on behalf of the Universal House of Justice to a National Spiritual Assembly **[43]**

77.   Letter dated 8 December 1967 written by the Universal House of Justice to an individual believer, cf. "Wellspring of Guidance", pp. 133-34 **[27]**

78.   ibid., p. 134 **[27]**

79.   Letter dated 24 September 1924 written by Shoghi Effendi to the
      Bahá'ís of America, published in "Bahá'í Administration: Selected
      Messages 1922-1932" (Wilmette: Bahá'í Publishing Trust, 1974), p.
      67 [1]

PROMOTING ENTRY BY TROOPS

A Compilation Prepared by the Research Department of the Universal
House of Justice
October 1993

The Bahá'í world needs to foster a united clarity of vision for the
expansion of the Cause and all its agencies, and a wide range of
activities suited to the differing conditions of both the general
population and the individual Bahá'ís. We therefore urge the friends,
and especially the Assemblies, to study this compilation, to
understand the coherence of its statements, and to use its counsels to
lend a renewed impetus to the spread of the Faith and the
establishment of the institutions of the Cause of God.

PROMOTING ENTRY BY TROOPS

From Letters Written by or on Behalf of Shoghi Effendi

1.   And now as I look into the future, I hope to see the friends at all times, in every land, and of every shade of thought and character, voluntarily and joyously rallying round their local and in particular their national centres of activity, upholding and promoting their interests with complete unanimity and contentment, with perfect understanding, genuine enthusiasm, and sustained vigour. This indeed is the one joy and yearning of my life, for it is the fountain-head from which all future blessings will flow, the broad foundation upon which the security of the Divine Edifice must ultimately rest. May we not hope that now at last the dawn of a brighter day is breaking upon our beloved Cause?

(24 September 1924, written by Shoghi Effendi to the Bahá'ís of America, published in "Bahá'í Administration: Selected Messages 1922-1932" (Wilmette: Bahá'í Publishing Trust, 1974), p. 67)

2.   The work that the members of your small family are doing in spreading the Cause and infusing its divine spirit among the people you meet, is a fact that no one familiar with your life can deny.... In time you will see how abundant the fruit of your services will be. It is not sufficient to number the souls that embrace the Cause to know the progress that it is making. The more important consequences of your activities are the spirit that is diffused into the life of the community, and the extent to which the teachings we proclaim become part of the consciousness and belief of the people that hear them. For it is only when the spirit has thoroughly permeated the world that the people will begin to enter the Faith in large numbers. At the beginning of spring only the few, exceptionally favoured seeds will sprout, but when the season gets in its full sway, and the atmosphere gets permeated with the warmth of true springtime, then masses of flowers will begin to appear, and a whole hillside suddenly blooms. We are still in the state when only isolated souls are awakened, but soon we shall have the full swing of the season and the quickening of whole groups and nations into the spiritual life breathed by Bahá'u'lláh.

(18 February 1932, written on behalf of Shoghi Effendi to an individual believer)

3.   ...with God's help, he trusts, you will succeed. He will surely reinforce your efforts and assist you in the completion of that task that lies before you. God will, however, assist us if we do our share and sacrifice in the path of the progress of His Faith. We have to feel the responsibility laid upon our shoulders, arise to carry it out, and then expect divine grace to be showered upon us.

(20 December 1932, written on behalf of Shoghi Effendi to a National Spiritual Assembly)

4.   Must humanity, tormented as she now is, be afflicted with still severer tribulations ere their purifying influence can prepare her to enter the heavenly Kingdom destined to be established upon earth? Must the inauguration of so vast, so unique, so illumined an era in human history be ushered in by so great a catastrophe in human affairs as to recall, nay surpass, the appalling collapse of Roman civilization in the first centuries of the Christian era? Must a series of profound convulsions stir and rock the human race ere Bahá'u'lláh can be enthroned in the hearts and consciences of the masses, ere His undisputed ascendency is universally recognized, and the noble edifice of His World Order is reared and established?

(11 March 1936, written by Shoghi Effendi, published in "The World Order of Bahá'u'lláh: Selected Letters" (Wilmette: Bahá'í Publishing Trust, 1991), pp. 201-2)

5.   Action inspired by confidence in the ultimate triumph of the Faith is, indeed, essential to the gradual and complete materialization of your hopes for the extension and consolidation of the Movement in your country. May the Almighty inspire each and every one of you with the zeal, determination, and faith to carry out His Will, and to proclaim His Message to those living in your land and beyond its confines.

(11 May 1934, written on behalf of Shoghi Effendi to an individual believer)

6.   From the record of its tumultuous history, almost every page of which portrays a fresh crisis, is laden with the description of a new calamity, recounts the tale of a base betrayal, and is sustained with the account of unspeakable atrocities, there emerges, clear and incontrovertible, the supreme truth that with every fresh outbreak of hostility to the Faith, whether from within or

from without, a corresponding measure of outpouring grace, sustaining its defenders and confounding its adversaries, has been providentially released, communicating a fresh impulse to the onward march of the Faith, while this impetus, in its turn, would, through its manifestations, provoke fresh hostility in quarters heretofore unaware of its challenging implications — this increased hostility being accompanied by a still more arresting revelation of Divine Power and a more abundant effusion of celestial grace, which, by enabling the upholders of that Faith to register still more brilliant victories, would thereby generate issues of still more vital import and raise up still more formidable enemies against a Cause that cannot but in the end resolve those issues and crush the resistance of those enemies, through a still more glorious unfoldment of its inherent power.

The resistless march of the Faith of Bahá'u'lláh, viewed in this light, and propelled by the stimulating influences which the unwisdom of its enemies and the force latent within itself both engender, resolves itself into a series of rhythmic pulsations, precipitated, on the one hand, through the explosive outbursts of its foes, and the vibrations of Divine Power, on the other, which speed it, with ever-increasing momentum, along that predestined course traced for it by the Hand of the Almighty.

(12 August 1941, postscript in the handwriting of Shoghi Effendi appended to a letter on his behalf, cf. "Messages to America: Selected Letters and Cablegrams Addressed to the Bahá'ís of North America, 1932-1946" (Wilmette: Bahá'í Publishing Committee, 1947), p. 51)

7.   If the friends always waited until they were fully qualified to do any particular task, the work of the Cause would be almost at a standstill! But the very act of striving to serve, however unworthy one may feel, attracts the blessings of God and enables one to become more fitted for the task.

(4 May 1942, written on behalf of Shoghi Effendi to an individual believer)

8.   Too great emphasis cannot be laid on the importance of the unity of the friends, for only by manifesting the greatness of their love for and patience with each other can they hope to attract large numbers to their ranks.

(2 August 1942, written on behalf of Shoghi Effendi to an individual believer)

9. He longs to see a greater degree of unity and love among the believers, for these are the spirit which must animate their Community life. Until the people of the world see a shining example set by us they will not embrace the Cause in masses, because they require to see the teachings demonstrated in a pattern of action.

    (13 March 1944, written on behalf of Shoghi Effendi to a Bahá'í winter school session)

10. Until the public sees in the Bahá'í Community a true pattern, in action, of something better than it already has, it will not respond to the Faith in large numbers.

    (13 March 1944, written on behalf of Shoghi Effendi to an individual believer)

11.   Dear Mr. and Mrs. ... have a great ability for kindling in the hearts the love of God. It is for this wholesome, warming, spiritualizing love that the world is thirsting today. The Bahá'ís will never succeed in attracting large numbers to the Faith until they see in our individual and community life acts, and the atmosphere, that bespeaks the love of God.

    (17 February 1945, written on behalf of Shoghi Effendi to an individual believer)

12. Above all, the healing Message of Bahá'u'lláh must, during the opening years of the second Bahá'í century, and through the instrumentality of an already properly functioning Administrative Order, whose ramifications have been extended to the four corners of the Western Hemisphere, be vividly, systematically brought to the attention of the masses, in their hour of grief, misery and confusion. A more audacious assertion of the challenging verities of the Faith; a more convincing presentation of its distinguishing truths; a fuller exposition of the character, the aims, and the achievements of its rising Administrative system, as the nucleus and pattern of its future world-embracing order; a more direct and intimate contact and association with the leaders of public thought whose activities and aims are akin to the teachings of Bahá'u'lláh, for the purpose of demonstrating the universality, the comprehensiveness, the liberality and the dynamic power of His Divine Message; a closer scrutiny of the ways and means wherby its claims can be vindicated, its defamers and detractors silenced, and its institutions

safeguarded; a more determined effort to exploit, to the fullest extent possible, the talents and abilities of the rank and file of the believers for the purpose of achieving these ends — these stand out as the paramount tasks summoning to a challenge, during these years of transition and turmoil, the entire body of the American believers. The facilities which the Radio and Press furnish must be utilized to a degree unprecedented in American Bahá'í history. The combined resources of the much-envied, exemplary American Bahá'í community must be harnessed for the effectual promotion of these meritorious purposes. Blessings, undreamt of in their scope and plenteousness, are bound to be vouchsafed to those who will, in these dark yet pregnant times, arise, to further these noble ends, and to hasten through their acts the hour at which a still more momentous stage in the evolution of a Divine and world-wide Plan can be launched.

(29 March 1945, postscript in the handwriting of Shoghi Effendi appended to a letter written on his behalf to a National Spiritual Assembly)

13.	There are two things which will contribute greatly to bringing more people into the Cause more swiftly: one is the maturity of the Bahá'ís within their Communities, functioning according to Bahá'í laws and in the proper spirit of unity, and the other is the disintegration of society and the suffering it will bring in its wake. When the old forms are seen to be hopelessly useless, the people will stir from their materialism and spiritual lethargy, and embrace the Faith.

(3 July 1948, written on behalf of Shoghi Effendi to an individual believer)

14.	There is nothing in the passage from the Master's Tablet on page 681, Volume III of His Tablets to lead us to believe the instant the Temple is entirely completed masses of people will embrace the Cause. They will; such a time will come; we hope it may be soon, but we cannot set a date for it. And such a statement certainly does not justify the friends to rest on their oars! On the contrary, they must pave the way, particularly within their ranks, for the reception of large numbers of believers. Let them put more effort into perfecting their purely Bahá'í relationships, become more united, more spiritually educated, more skilled in fulfilling their administrative tasks, as a preparation to teaching and welcoming larger numbers of new believers.

(25 March 1949, written on behalf of Shoghi Effendi to an individual believer)

15. Without the spirit of real love for Bahá'u'lláh, for His Faith and its Institutions, and the believers for each other, the Cause can never really bring in large numbers of people. For it is not preaching and rules the world wants, but love and action.

(25 October 1949, written on behalf of Shoghi Effendi to an individual believer)

16.   Although tremendous progress has been made in the United States during the last quarter of a century, he feels that the believers must ever-increasingly become aware of the fact that only to the degree that they mirror forth in their joint lives the exalted standards of the Faith will they attract the masses to the Cause of God.

(15 September 1951, written on behalf of Shoghi Effendi to a Bahá'í school session)

17.   The Latin American communities are still on the threshold of their international Bahá'í life; he feels sure that they will rapidly grow into it. Compared with the length of time it took the North American, the British, and the French communities to grow up and spread, their growth is like lightning. As the Cause spreads all over the world its rate of acceleration increases, too, and new centres in Africa, in some mysterious way, have spiritual repercussions which aid in forming new centres everywhere.

(30 June 1952, written on behalf of Shoghi Effendi to a National Spiritual Assembly)

18.   Such a steady flow of reinforcements is absolutely vital and is of extreme urgency, for nothing short of the vitalizing influx of new blood that will reanimate the world Bahá'í Community can safeguard the prizes which, at so great a sacrifice, involving the expenditure of so much time, effort and treasure, are now being won in virgin territories by Bahá'u'lláh's valiant Knights, whose privilege is to constitute the spearhead of the onrushing battalions which, in divers theatres and in circumstances often adverse and extremely challenging, are vying with each other for the spiritual conquest of the unsurrendered territories and islands on the surface of the globe.

This flow, moreover, will presage and hasten the advent of the day which, as prophesied by 'Abdu'l-Bahá, will witness the entry by troops of peoples of divers nations and races into the Bahá'í world — a day which, viewed in its proper perspective, will be the prelude to that long-awaited hour when a mass conversion on the part of these same nations and races, and as a direct result of a chain of events, momentous and possibly catastrophic in nature and which cannot as yet be even dimly visualized, will suddenly revolutionize the fortunes of the Faith, derange the equilibrium of the world, and reinforce a thousandfold the numerical strength as well as the material power and the spiritual authority of the Faith of Bahá'u'lláh.

(25 June 1953, written by Shoghi Effendi, published in "Citadel of Faith: Messages to America 1947-1957" (Wilmette: Bahá'í Publishing Trust, 1980), p. 117)*

19. This is the ebb of the tide. The Bahá'ís know that the tide will turn and come in, after mankind has suffered, with mighty waves of faith and devotion. Then people will enter the Cause of God in troops, and the whole condition will change. The Bahá'ís see this new condition which will take place, as one on a mountaintop sees the first glimpse of the dawn, before others are aware of it; and it is toward this that the Bahá'ís must work.

(5 October 1953, written on behalf of Shoghi Effendi to an individual believer)

20. When the true spirit of teaching, which calls for complete dedication, consecration to the noble mission, and living the life, is fulfilled, not only by the individuals, but by the Assemblies also, then the Faith will grow by leaps and bounds.

(19 March 1954, written on behalf of Shoghi Effendi to a Local Spiritual Assembly)

21. The Crusade, on which the army of the Lord of Hosts has so joyously and confidently embarked, now stands at a major turning point in the history of its marvellous unfoldment. Three years of magnificent exploits, achieved for the propagation of the light of an immortal and infinitely precious Faith and for the strengthening of the fabric of its Administrative Order, now lie behind it. A spirit of abnegation and self-sacrifice, so rare that only the spirit of the

---

* Published version gives date as 18 July 1953.

Dawn-breakers of a former age can be said to have surpassed it, has consistently animated, singly as well as collectively, its participants in every clime, of all classes, of either sex, and of every age. A treasure, immense in its range, has been willingly and lovingly expended to ensure its systematic and successful prosecution. Already a few heroic souls have either quaffed the cup of martyrdom, or laid down their lives, or been subjected to divers ordeals while combatting for its Cause. Its repercussions have spread so far as to alarm a not inconsiderable element among the traditional and redoubtable adversaries of its courageous and consecrated prosecutors. Indeed as it has forged ahead, it has raised up new enemies intent on obstructing its forward march and on defeating its purpose. Premonitory signs can already be discerned in far-off regions heralding the approach of the day when troops will flock to its standard, fulfilling the predictions uttered long ago by the Supreme Captain of its forces.

(April 1956, written by Shoghi Effendi to all National Spiritual Assemblies)

22.   The steady progress achieved in recent years by both the Swiss and Italian Bahá'í communities, unitedly labouring with exemplary fidelity and devotion for the propagation of the Faith of Bahá'u'lláh, has greatly encouraged me and brought much happiness to my heart, and has, no doubt, heightened the admiration of their sister communities for the manner in which they are acquitting themselves of their arduous and sacred tasks....

Less substantial, however, has been the progress achieved in the all-important teaching field, and far inferior the acceleration in the vital process of individual conversion for which the entire machinery of the Administrative Order has been primarily and so laboriously erected.

(12 August 1957, postscript in the handwriting of Shoghi Effendi appended to a letter written on his behalf to a National Spiritual Assembly)

From Letters Written by or on Behalf of the Universal House of Justice

23.   When the masses of mankind are awakened and enter the Faith of God, a new process is set in motion and the growth of a new civilization begins. Witness the emergence of Christianity and of Islám. These masses are the rank and file, steeped in traditions of their own, but receptive to the new Word of God, by which, when they truly respond to it, they become so influenced as to transform those who come in contact with them.

...In countries where teaching the masses has succeeded, the Bahá'ís have poured out their time and effort in village areas to the same extent as they had formerly done in cities and towns. The results indicate how unwise it is to solely concentrate on one section of the population. Each National Spiritual Assembly therefore should so balance its resources and harmonize its efforts that the Faith of God is taught not only to those who are readily accessible but to all sections of society, however remote they may be....

When teaching among the masses, the friends should be careful not to emphasize the charitable and humanitarian aspects of the Faith as a means to win recruits. Experience has shown that when facilities such as schools, dispensaries, hospitals, or even clothes and food are offered to the people being taught, many complications arise. The prime motive should always be the response of man to God's message, and the recognition of His Messenger....

Expansion and consolidation are twin processes that must go hand in hand. The friends must not stop expansion in the name of consolidation. Deepening the newly enrolled believers generates tremendous stimulus which results in further expansion. The enrolment of new believers, on the other hand, creates a new spirit in the community and provides additional potential man-power that will reinforce the consolidation work.

(13 July 1964, written by the Universal House of Justice to all National Spiritual Assemblies, cf. "Wellspring of Guidance: Messages 1963-1968" (Wilmette: Bahá'í Publishing Trust, 1976), pp. 31-33)

24.   The second challenge facing us is to raise the intensity of teaching to a pitch never before attained, in order to realize that "vast increase" called for in the Plan. Universal participation and constant action will win this goal. Every believer has a part to play, and is capable of playing it, for every soul meets others, and, as promised by Bahá'u'lláh, "Whosoever ariseth to aid Our Cause God will render him victorious...." The confusion of the world is not diminishing, rather does it increase with each passing day, and men and women are losing faith in human remedies. Realization is at last dawning that "There is no place to flee to" save God. Now is the golden opportunity; people are willing, in many places eager, to listen to the divine remedy.

(Riḍván 1965 message written by the Universal House of Justice to the
Bahá'ís of the world)

25.   It has been due to the splendid victories in large-scale conversion that the
Faith of Bahá'u'lláh has entered a new phase in its development and
establishment throughout the world. It is imperative, therefore, that the
process of teaching the masses be not only maintained but accelerated. The
teaching committee structure that each National Assembly may adopt to
ensure best results in the extension of its teaching work is a matter left entirely
to its discretion, but an efficient teaching structure there must be, so that the
tasks are carried out with dispatch and in accordance with the administrative
principles of our Faith. From among the believers native to each country,
competent travelling teachers must be selected and teaching projects worked
out....

While this vital teaching work is progressing each National Assembly
must ever bear in mind that expansion and consolidation are inseparable
processes that must go hand in hand.... To ensure that the spiritual life of the
individual believer is continuously enriched, that local communities are
becoming increasingly conscious of their collective duties, and that the
institutions of an evolving administration are operating efficiently, is,
therefore, as important as expanding into new fields and bringing in the
multitudes under the shadow of the Cause.

(2 February 1966, written by the Universal House of Justice to all
National Spiritual Assemblies engaged in mass teaching work)

26.   The paramount goal of the teaching work at the present time is to carry
the message of Bahá'u'lláh to every stratum of human society and every walk
of life. An eager response to the teachings will often be found in the most
unexpected quarters, and any such response should be quickly followed up,
for success in a fertile area awakens a response in those who were at first
uninterested.

The same presentation of the teachings will not appeal to everybody; the
method of expression and the approach must be varied in accordance with the
outlook and interests of the hearer. An approach which is designed to appeal
to everybody will usually result in attracting the middle section, leaving both
extremes untouched. No effort must be spared to ensure that the healing Word
of God reaches the rich and the poor, the learned and the illiterate, the old and

the young, the devout and the atheist, the dweller in the remote hills and islands, the inhabitants of the teeming cities, the suburban businessman, the labourer in the slums, the nomadic tribesman, the farmer, the university student; all must be brought consciously within the teaching plans of the Bahá'í Community.

Whereas plans must be carefully made, and every useful means adopted in the furtherance of this work, your Assemblies must never let such plans eclipse the shining truth expounded in the enclosed quotations: that it is the purity of heart, detachment, uprightness, devotion and love of the teacher that attracts the divine confirmations and enables him, however ignorant he be in this world's learning, to win the hearts of his fellowmen to the Cause of God.

(31 October 1967, written by the Universal House of Justice to all National Spiritual Assemblues, cf. "Wellspring of Guidance", pp. 124-25)

27.   We are told by Shoghi Effendi that two great processes are at work in the world: the great Plan of God, tumultuous in its progress, working through mankind as a whole, tearing down barriers to world unity and forging humankind into a unified body in the fires of suffering and experience. This process will produce, in God's due time, the Lesser Peace, the political unification of the world. Mankind at that time can be likened to a body that is unified but without life. The second process, the task of breathing life into this unified body — of creating true unity and spirituality culminating in the Most Great Peace — is that of the Bahá'ís, who are labouring consciously, with detailed instructions and continuing divine guidance, to erect the fabric of the Kingdom of God on earth, into which they call their fellow-men, thus conferring upon them eternal life.

The working out of God's Major Plan proceeds mysteriously in ways directed by Him alone, but the Minor Plan that He has given us to execute, as our part in His grand design for the redemption of mankind, is clearly delineated. It is to this work that we must devote all our energies, for there is no one else to do it.

(8 December 1967, written by the Universal House of Justice to an individual believer, cf. "Wellspring of Guidance", pp. 133-34)

28. Wherever a Bahá'í community exists, whether large or small, let it be distinguished for its abiding sense of security and faith, its high standard of rectitude, its complete freedom from all forms of prejudice, the spirit of love among its members and for the closely knit fabric of its social life. The acute distinction between this and present-day society will inevitably arouse the interest of the more enlightened, and as the world's gloom deepens the light of Bahá'í life will shine even brighter and brighter until its brilliance must eventually attract the disillusioned masses and cause them to enter the haven of the Covenant of Bahá'u'lláh, Who alone can bring them peace and justice and an ordered life.

(August 1968, message written by the Universal House of Justice to the Palermo Conference, cf. "Messages from the Universal House of Justice, 1968-1973" (Wilmette: Bahá'í Publishing Trust, 1976), p. 12)

29.   We note that the new teaching methods you have developed, in reaching the waiting masses, have substantially influenced the winning of your goals, and we urge the American Bahá'ís, one and all, newly enrolled and believers of long standing, to arise, put their reliance in Bahá'u'lláh and armed with that supreme power, continue unabated their efforts to reach the waiting souls, while simultaneously consolidating the hard-won victories. New methods inevitably bring with them criticism and challenges no matter how successful they may ultimately prove to be. The influx of so many new believers is, in itself, a call to the veteran believers to join the ranks of those in this field of service and to give wholeheartedly of their knowledge and experience. Far from standing aloof, the American believers are called upon now, as never before, to grasp this golden opportunity which has been presented to them, to consult together prayerfully and widen the scope of their endeavours.

Efforts to reach the minorities should be increased and broadened to include all minority groups such as the Indians, Spanish-speaking people, Japanese and Chinese. Indeed, every stratum of American society must be reached and can be reached with the healing Message, if the believers will but arise and go forth with the spirit which is conquering the citadels of the southern states. Such a programme, coupled as it must be with continuous consolidation, can be effectively carried out by universal participation on the part of every lover of Bahá'u'lláh.

(14 February 1972, written by the Universal House of Justice to the National Spiritual Assembly of the United States, published in "Messages from the Universal House of Justice, 1968-1973", pp. 85-86)

30.   Strengthening and development of Local Spiritual Assemblies is a vital objective of the Five Year Plan. Success in this one goal will greatly enrich the quality of Bahá'í life, will heighten the capacity of the Faith to deal with entry by troops which is even now taking place and, above all, will demonstrate the solidarity and ever-growing distinctiveness of the Bahá'í community, thereby attracting more and more thoughtful souls to the Faith and offering a refuge to the leaderless and hapless millions of the spiritually bankrupt, moribund present order.

(Naw-Rúz 1974 message written by the Universal House of Justice to the Bahá'ís of the world)

31.   Teaching the Faith embraces many diverse activities, all of which are vital to success, and each of which reinforces the other....

The aim, therefore, of all Bahá'í institutions and Bahá'í teachers is to advance continually to new areas and strata of society, with such thoroughness that, as the spark of faith kindles the hearts of the hearers, the teaching of the believers continues until, and even after, they shoulder their responsibilities as Bahá'ís and participate in both the teaching and administrative work of the Faith.

There are now many areas in the world where thousands of people have accepted the Faith so quickly that it has been beyond the capacity of the existing communities to consolidate adequately these advances. The people in these areas must be progressively deepened in their understanding of the Faith, in accordance with well-laid plans, so that their communities may, as soon as possible, become sources of great strength to the work of the Faith and begin to manifest the pattern of Bahá'í life.

(25 May 1975, written by the Universal House of Justice to all National Spiritual Assemblies)

32.   In many lands, however, there is an eager receptivity for the teachings of the Faith. The challenge for the Bahá'ís is to provide these thousands of seeking souls, as swiftly as possible, with the spiritual food that they crave, to enlist them under the banner of Bahá'u'lláh, to nurture them in the way of life He has revealed, and to guide them to elect Local Spiritual Assemblies which, as they begin to function strongly, will unite the friends in firmly consolidated Bahá'í communities and become beacons of guidance and havens of refuge to mankind....

Throughout the world the Seven Year Plan must witness the attainment of the following objectives:...

–   The teaching work, both that organized by institutions of the Faith and that which is the fruit of individual initiative, must be actively carried forward so that there will be growing numbers of believers, leading more countries to the stage of entry by troops and ultimately to mass conversion.

–   This teaching work must include prompt, thorough and continuing consolidation so that all victories will be safeguarded, the number of Local Spiritual Assemblies will be increased and the foundations of the Cause reinforced.

(Naw-Rúz 1979 message written by the Universal House of Justice to the Bahá'ís of the world)

33.   The Faith of God does not advance at one uniform pace. Sometimes it is like the advance of the sea when the tide is rising. Meeting a sandbank the water seems to be held back, but, with a new wave, it surges forward, flooding past the barrier which checked it for a little while. If the friends will but persist in their efforts, the cumulative effect of years of work will suddenly appear.

(27 July 1980, written by the Universal House of Justice to a National Spiritual Assembly)

34.   The ... problem occurs most frequently in countries such as those in Africa, where there is entry by troops. In such countries it is comparatively easy to bring large numbers of new believers into the Faith, and this is such a thrilling experience that visiting teachers often tend to prefer to do this rather than help with the consolidation work.... It should be pointed out that, especially if they [the travelling teachers] are assigned to expansion work, they must remember that consolidation is an essential and inseparable element of teaching, and if they go to a remote area and enrol believers whom no one is going to be able to visit again in the near future, they may well be doing a disservice to those people and to the Faith. To give people this glorious Message and then to leave them in the lurch, produces disappointment and disillusionment, so that, when it does become possible to carry out properly planned teaching in that area, the teachers may well find the people resistant to the Message. The first teacher who was careless of consolidation, instead of planting and nourishing the seeds of faith has, in fact, "inoculated" the people against the Divine Message and made subsequent teaching very much harder.

(16 April 1981, written on behalf of the Universal House of Justice to all Continental Pioneer Committees)

35. Consolidation is as vital a part of the teaching work as expansion. It is that aspect of teaching which assists the believers to deepen their knowledge and understanding of the Teachings, and fans the flame of their devotion to Bahá'u'lláh and His Cause, so that they will, of their own volition, continue the process of their spiritual development, promote the teaching work, and strengthen the functioning of their administrative institutions. Proper consolidation is essential to the preservation of the spiritual health of the community, to the protection of its interests, to the upholding of its good name, and ultimately to the continuation of the work of expansion itself.

(17 April 1981, written on behalf of the Universal House of Justice to all National Spiritual Assemblies)

36. Who can doubt that we are now entering a period of unprecedented and unimaginable developments in the onward march of the Faith?... We know that the present victories will lead to active opposition, for which the Bahá'í world community must be prepared. We know the prime needs of the Cause at the moment: a vast expansion of its numbers and financial resources; a greater consolidation of its community life and the authority of its institutions; an observable increase in those characteristics of loving unity, stability of family life, freedom from prejudice and rectitude of conduct which must distinguish the Bahá'ís from the spiritually lost and wayward multitudes around them. Surely the time cannot be long delayed when we must deal universally with that entry by troops foretold by the Master as a prelude to mass conversion.

(27 December 1985, message written by the Universal House of Justice to the Conference of the Continental Boards of Counsellors)

37. The House of Justice read with much interest the circumstances which inspired the new impetus being experienced in your teaching activities and was happy to learn that the ... believers are themselves taking a more active part in the teaching work. This trend should by all means be encouraged by your Assembly, which should do everything in its power to ensure that increasing numbers of native believers are deepened in the verities of the Faith and encouraged to teach not only through the means recently opened to them, but through the variety of approaches which are possible in different parts of the country and among different strata of ... society. While taking the fullest advantage of a workable method in one area, the friends should be open to other methods and not blindly insist upon doing the same thing everywhere. If such flexibility is understood, your community will surely grow in numbers and strength.

(13 November 1986, written on behalf of the Universal House of Justice to a National Spiritual Assembly)

38.   The stage is set for universal, rapid and massive growth of the Cause of God.... The all-important teaching work must be imaginatively, persistently and sacrificially continued, ensuring the enrolment of ever larger numbers who will provide the energy, the resources and spiritual force to enable the beloved Cause to worthily play its part in the redemption of mankind.

(Riḍván 1987 message written by the Universal House of Justice to the Bahá'ís of the world)

39. The Faith advances, not at a uniform rate of growth, but in vast surges, precipitated by the alternation of crisis and victory. In a passage written on 18 July 1953, in the early months of the Ten Year Crusade, Shoghi Effendi, referring to the vital need to ensure through the teaching work a "steady flow" of "fresh recruits to the slowly yet steadily advancing army of the Lord of Hosts", stated that this flow would "presage and hasten the advent of the day which, as prophesied by 'Abdu'l-Bahá, will witness the entry by troops of peoples of divers nations and races into the Bahá'í world". This day the Bahá'í world has already seen in Africa, the Pacific, in Asia and in Latin America, and this process of entry by troops must, in the present plan, be augmented and spread to other countries for, as the Guardian stated in this same letter, it "will be the prelude to that long-awaited hour when a mass conversion on the part of these same nations and races, and as a direct result of a chain of events, momentous and possibly catastrophic in nature, and which cannot as yet be even dimly visualized, will suddenly revolutionize the fortunes of the Faith, derange the equilibrium of the world, and reinforce a thousandfold the numerical strength as well as the material power and the spiritual authority of the Faith of Bahá'u'lláh". This is the time for which we must now prepare ourselves; this is the hour whose coming it is our task to hasten.

(31 August 1987, written by the Universal House of Justice to the Bahá'ís of the world)

40.   A silver lining to the dark picture which has overshadowed most of this century now brightens the horizon. It is discernible in the new tendencies impelling the social processes at work throughout the world, in the evidences of an accelerated trend towards peace. In the Faith of God, it is the growing strength of the Order of Bahá'u'lláh as its banner rises to more stately heights. It is a strength that attracts. The media are giving increasing attention to the Bahá'í world community; authors are acknowledging its existence in a growing number of articles, books and reference works, one of the most highly respected of which recently listed the Faith as the most widely spread religion after Christianity. A remarkable display of interest in this community by governments, civil authorities, prominent personalities and humanitarian organizations is increasingly apparent. Not only are the community's laws and principles, organization and way of life being investigated, but its advice and active help are also being sought for the alleviation of social problems and the carrying out of humanitarian activities.

The spark which ignited the mounting interest in the Cause of Bahá'u'lláh was the heroic fortitude and patience of the beloved friends in Irán, which moved the Bahá'í world community to conduct a persistent, carefully orchestrated programme of appeal to the conscience of the world. This vast undertaking, involving the entire community acting unitedly through its Administrative Order, was accompanied by equally vigorous and visible

A thrilling consequence of these favourably conjoined developments is the emergence of a new paradigm of opportunity for further growth and consolidation of our world-wide community. New prospects for teaching the Cause at all levels of society have unfolded. These are confirmed in the early results flowing from the new teaching initiatives being fostered in a number of places as more and more national communities witness the beginnings of that entry by troops promised by the beloved Master and which Shoghi Effendi said would lead on to mass conversion. The immediate possibilities presented by this providential situation compel us to expect that an expansion of the Community of the Most Great Name, such as has not yet been experienced, is, indeed, at hand.

activities of that community in other spheres which have been detailed separately. Nonetheless, we are impelled to mention that an important outcome of this extensive exertion is our recognition of a new stage in the external affairs of the Cause, characterized by a marked maturation of National Spiritual Assemblies in their growing relations with governmental and non-governmental organizations and with the public in general....

But the paramount purpose of all Bahá'í activity is teaching. All that has been done or will be done revolves around this central activity, the "head corner-stone of the foundation itself", to which all progress in the Cause is due. The present challenge calls for teaching on a scale and of a quality, a variety, and intensity outstripping all current efforts. The time is now, lest opportunity be lost in the swiftly changing moods of a frenetic world. Let it not be imagined that expedience is the essential motive arousing this sense of urgency. There is an overarching reason: it is the pitiful plight of masses of humanity, suffering and in turmoil, hungering after righteousness, but "bereft of discernment to see God with there own eyes, or hear His Melody with their own ears". They must be fed. Vision must be restored where hope is lost, confidence built where doubt and confusion are rife. In these and other respects, "The Promise of World Peace" is designed to open the way. Its delivery to national governmental leaders having been virtually completed, its contents must now be conveyed, by all possible means, to peoples everywhere from all walks of life. This is a necessary part of the teaching work in our time and must be pursued with unabated vigour.

Teaching is the food of the spirit; it brings life to unawakened souls and raises the new heaven and the new earth; it uplifts the banner of a unified world; it ensures the victory of the Covenant and brings those who give their lives to it the supernal happiness of attainment to the good pleasure of their Lord.

Every individual believer — man, woman, youth and child — is summoned to this field of action; for it is on the initiative, the resolute will of the individual to teach and to serve, that the success of the entire community depends. Well-grounded in the mighty Covenant of Bahá'u'lláh, sustained by daily prayer and reading of the Holy Word, strengthened by a continual striving to obtain a deeper understanding of the divine Teachings, illumined by a constant endeavour to relate these Teachings to current issues, nourished by observance of the laws and principles of His wondrous World Order, every individual can attain increasing measures of success in teaching. In sum, the ultimate triumph of the Cause is assured by that "one thing and only one thing" so poignantly emphasized by Shoghi Effendi, namely, "the extent to which our own inner life and private character mirror forth in their manifold aspects the spendour of those eternal principles proclaimed by Bahá'u'lláh".

(Riḍván 1988 message written by the Universal House of Justice to the Bahá'ís of the world)

41. Your concern about consolidation and "mass teaching" is noted. The concept of mass teaching may be better understood if put in the context of "teaching the masses". This implies reaching every level of society in every continent and island in the world. In developing countries large segments of the population have become Bahá'ís, usually among the less educated. More recently, particularly in Asia, we see that the youth in high schools and colleges have been attracted to the Faith in large numbers. This does not mean, however, that there is any particular system of teaching which individual Bahá'ís should pursue. Different cultures and types of people require different methods of approach. While taking the fullest advantage of a workable method in one area, the friends should be open to other methods and not blindly insist upon doing the same thing everywhere. If such flexibility is understood, the ... community will surely grow in numbers and strength.

(11 August 1988, written on behalf of the Universal House of Justice to an individual believer)

42. What is required is a sense of urgency in **teaching** and this means to ignite the spark of faith and devotion in the hearts of the people and fan it so that those who accept the Faith become its firm and ardent supporters. Inevitably some of those who are attracted to the Message and declare their acceptance of it will later drift away from the Cause — this is in the nature of the human response to all teachings — but the effort of the Bahá'ís should be to teach not only as intensively as possible but also as well as possible.

(1 November 1988, written on behalf of the Universal House of Justice to a National Spiritual Assembly)

43. The International Teaching Centre has concluded that the Bahá'í institutions in ... seem to have been placing too much reliance on large, expensive projects, involving a great deal of successful public relations and proclamation. These are, in their own way, very useful activities, but it must be realized that they cannot be expected to produce large numbers of new believers. The key to the conversion of people to the Faith is the action of the individual Bahá'í conveying the spark of faith to individual seekers, answering their questions and deepening their understanding of the teachings.

(9 February 1989, written on behalf of the Universal House of Justice to a National Spiritual Assembly)

44.   The spiritual current which exerted such galvanic effects at the International Bahá'í Convention last Riḍván has swept through the entire world community, arousing its members in both the East and the West to feats of activity and achievement in teaching never before experienced in any one year. The high level of enrolments alone bears this out, as nearly half a million new believers have already been reported. The names of such far-flung places as India and Liberia, Bolivia and Bangladesh, Taiwan and Peru, the Philippines and Haiti leap to the fore as we contemplate the accumulating evidences of the entry by troops called for in our message of a year ago. These are hopeful signs of the greater acceleration yet to come and in which all national communities, whatever the current status of their teaching effort, will ultimately be involved....

All these requirements must and will surely be met through reconsecrated service on the part of every conscientous member of the Community of Bahá, and particularly through personal commitment to the teaching work. So fundamentally important is this work to ensuring the foundation for success in all Bahá'í undertakings and to furthering the process of entry by troops that we are moved to add a word of emphasis for your consideration. It is not enough to proclaim the Bahá'í message, essential as that is. It is not enough to expand the rolls of Bahá'í membership, vital as that is. Souls must be transformed, communities thereby consolidated, new models of life thus attained. Transformation is the essential purpose of the Cause of Bahá'u'lláh, but it lies in the will and effort of the individual to achieve it in obedience to the Covenant. Necessary to the progress of this life-fulfilling transformation is knowledge of the will and purpose of God through regular reading and study of the Holy Word.

Beloved Friends: The momentum generated by this past year's achievements is reflected not only in the opportunities for marked expansion of the Cause but also in a broad range of challenges — momentous, insistent and varied — which have combined in ways that place demands beyond any previous measure upon our spiritual and material resources. We must be prepared to meet them. At this mid-point of the Six Year Plan, we have reached a historic moment pregnant with hopes and possibilities — a moment at which significant trends in the world are becoming more closely aligned with principles and objectives of the Cause of God. The urgency upon our community to press onward in fulfilment of its world-embracing mission is therefore tremendous.

Our primary response must be to teach — teach ourselves and to teach others — at all levels of society, by all possible means, and without further delay.

(Riḍván 1989 message written by the Universal House of Justice to the Bahá'ís of the world)

45. Over the last two years, almost one million souls entered the Cause. The increasing instances of entry by troops in different places contributed to that growth, drawing attention to Shoghi Effendi's vision which shapes our perception of glorious future possibilities in the teaching field. For he has asserted that the process of "entry by troops of peoples of divers nations and races into the Bahá'í world ... will be the prelude to that long-awaited hour when a mass conversion on the part of these same nations and races, and as a direct result of a chain of events, momentous and possibly catastrophic in nature, and which cannot as yet be even dimly visualized, will suddenly revolutionize the fortunes of the Faith, derange the equilibrium of the world, and reinforce a thousandfold the numerical strength as well as the material power and the spiritual authority of the Faith of Bahá'u'lláh". We have every encouragement to believe that large-scale enrolments will expand, involving village after village, town after town, from one country to another. However, it is not for us to wait passively for the ultimate fulfilment of Shoghi Effendi's vision. We few, placing our whole trust in the providence of God and regarding as a divine privilege the challenges which face us, must proceed to victory with the plans in hand.

An expansion of thought and action in certain aspects of our work would enhance our possibilities for success in meeting our aforementioned commitments. Since change, ever more rapid change, is a constant characteristic of life at this time, and since our growth, size and external relations demand much of us, our community must be ready to adapt. In a sense this means that the community must become more adept at accommodating a wide range of actions without losing concentration on the primary objectives of teaching, namely, expansion and consolidation. A unity in diversity of actions is called for, a condition in which different individuals will concentrate on different activities, appreciating the salutary effect of the aggregate on the growth and development of the Faith, because each person cannot do everything and all persons cannot do the same thing. This understanding is important to the maturity which, by the many demands being made upon it, the community is being forced to attain.

The Order brought by Bahá'u'lláh is intended to guide the progress and resolve the problems of society. Our numbers are as yet too small to effect an adequate demonstration of the potentialities inherent in the administrative system we are building, and the efficacy of this system will not be fully appreciated without a vast expansion of our membership. With the prevailing situation in the world the necessity to effect such a demonstration becomes more compelling. It is all too obvious that even those who rail against the defects of the old order, and would even tear it down, are themselves bereft of any viable alternative to put in its place. Since the Administrative Order is designed to be a pattern for future society, the visibility of such a pattern will be a signal of hope to those who despair.

Thus far, we have achieved a marvellous diversity in the large numbers of ethnic groups represented in the Faith, and everything should be done to fortify it through larger enrolments from among groups already represented and the attraction of members from groups not yet reached. However, there is another category of diversity which must be built up and without which the Cause will not be able adequately to meet the challenges being thrust upon it. Its membership, regardless of ethnic variety, needs now to embrace increasing numbers of people of capacity, including persons of accomplishment and prominence in the various fields of human endeavour. Enrolling significant numbers of such persons is an indispensible aspect of teaching the masses, an aspect which cannot any longer be neglected and which must be consciously and deliberately incorporated into our teaching work, so as to broaden its base and accelerate the process of entry by troops. So important and timely is the need for action on this matter that we are impelled to call upon Continental Counsellors and National Spiritual Assemblies to devote serious attention to it in their consultations and plans.

The affairs of mankind have reached a stage at which increasing calls will be made upon our community to assist, through advice and practical measures, in solving critical social problems. It is a service that we will gladly render, but this means that our Local and National Spiritual Assemblies must adhere more scrupulously to principle. With increasing public attention being focused on the Cause of God, it becomes imperative for Bahá'í institutions to improve their performance, through a closer identification with the fundamental verities of the Faith, through greater conformity to the spirit and form of Bahá'í administration and through a keener reliance on the beneficial effects of proper consultation, so that the communities they guide will reflect a pattern of life that will offer hope to the disillusioned members of society.

That there are indications that the Lesser Peace cannot be too far distant, that the local and national institutions of the Administrative Order are growing steadily in experience and influence, that the plans for the construction of the remaining administrative edifices on the Arc are in an advanced stage — that these hopeful conditions make more discernible the shaping of the dynamic synchronization envisaged by Shoghi Effendi, no honest observer can deny.

As a community clearly in the vanguard of the constructive forces at work on the planet, and as one which has access to proven knowledge, let us be about our Father's business. He will, from His glorious retreats on high, release liberal effusions of His grace upon our humble efforts, astonishing us with the incalculable victories of His conquering power. It is for the unceasing blessings of such a Father that we shall continue to supplicate on behalf of each and every one of you at the Sacred Threshold.

(Riḍván 1990 message written by the Universal House of Justice to the
Bahá'ís of the world)

46. Above all, it is essential for the friends to have the confidence that a new receptivity is dawning in the hearts of Europeans, and to have faith that the seeds they sow will germinate. They must know that the time is coming when the number of their fellow-countrymen who accept the Faith will suddenly increase, and they must be ready and eager to welcome these new believers.

(12 September 1991, written on behalf of the Universal House of Justice to
a National Spiritual Assembly)

47. All these developments have made it evident that the accumulated potential for further progress of the Bahá'í community is incalculable. The changed situation within and among nations and the many problems afflicting society amplify this potential. The impression produced by such change is of the near approach of the Lesser Peace. But there has been a simultaneous recrudescence of countervailing forces. With the fresh tide of political freedom resulting from the collapse of the strongholds of communism has come an explosion of nationalism. The concomitant rise of racism in many regions has become a matter of serious global concern. These are compounded by an upsurge in religious fundamentalism which is poisoning the wells of tolerance. Terrorism is rife. Widespread uncertainty about the condition of the economy indicates a deep disorder in the management of the material affairs of the planet, a condition which can only exacerbate the sense of frustration and futility affecting the political realm. The worsening state of the environment and of the health of huge populations is a source of alarm. And yet an element of this change is the amazing advances in communications technology making possible the rapid transmission of information and ideas from one part of the world to the other. It is against such "simultaneous processes of rise and fall, of integration and of disintegration, of order and chaos, with their continuous and reciprocal reactions on each other", that a myriad new opportunities for the next stage in the unfoldment of the beloved Master's Divine Plan present themselves.

The burgeoning influence of Bahá'u'lláh's Revelation seemed, with the imminence of the Holy Year, to have assumed the character of an onrushing wind blowing through the archaic structures of the old order, felling mighty pillars and clearing the ground for new conceptions of social organization. The call for unity, for a new world order, is audible from many directions. The change in world society is characterized by a phenomenal speed. A feature of this change is a suddenness, or precipitateness, which appears to be the consequence of some mysterious, rampant force. The positive aspects of this change reveal an unaccustomed openness to global concepts, movement towards international and regional collaboration, an inclination of warring parties to opt for peaceful solutions, a search for spiritual values. Even the Community of the Most Great Name itself is experiencing the rigorous effects of this quickening wind as it ventilates the modes of thought of us all, renewing, clarifying and amplifying our perspectives as to the purpose of the Order of Bahá'u'lláh in the wake of humanity's suffering and turmoil.

The situation in the world, while presenting us with an acute challenge of the utmost urgency, calls to mind the encouraging global vision of Shoghi Effendi for the prospects of the Administrative Order during the second century of the Bahá'í Era, whose midpoint we are rapidly approaching. In

1946, he wrote: "The second century is destined to witness a tremendous deployment and a notable consolidation of the forces working towards the world-wide development of that Order, as well as the first stirrings of that World Order, of which the present Administrative System is at once the precursor, the nucleus and pattern — an Order which, as it slowly crystallizes and radiates its benign influence over the entire planet, will proclaim at once the coming of age of the whole human race, as well as the maturity of the Faith itself, the progenitor of that Order."

(Ridván 1992 message written by the Universal House of Justice to the Bahá'ís of the world)

48. The centennial year was also a period in which the situation in the world at large became more confused and paradoxical: there were simultaneous signs of order and chaos, promise and frustration. Amid the convolutions of the current global state of affairs, but with such feelings of wonder and joy, courage and faith as the Holy Year has induced in our hearts, we, at this Ridván, in the one hundred and fiftieth year of our Faith, are embarked upon a Three Year Plan. Its brevity is compelled by the swiftly changing tides of the times. But the Plan's primary purpose is indispensable to the future of the Cause and of humankind. It is the next stage in the unfoldment of the divine charter of teaching penned by the Centre of the Covenant. The Plan will be a measure of our determination to respond to the immense opportunities at this critical moment in the social evolution of the planet. Through resolute pursuit of its stated objectives and full realization of its goals, as suited to the circumstances of each national community, the way will be made clear for a fit projection of the role of the Faith in relation to the inevitable challenges facing all humanity towards the end of the fast fleeting, fate-laden twentieth century.

A massive expansion of the Bahá'í community must be achieved far beyond all past records. The task of spreading the Message to the generality of mankind in villages, towns and cities must be rapidly extended. The need for this is critical, for without it the laboriously erected agencies of the Administrative Order will not be provided the scope to be able to develop and adequately demonstrate their inherent capacity to minister to the crying needs of humanity in its hour of deepening despair. In this regard the mutuality of teaching and administration must be fully understood and widely emphasized, for each reinforces the other. The problems of society which affect our community and those problems which naturally arise from within the community itself, whether social, spiritual, economic or administrative, will be solved as our numbers and resources multiply, and as at all levels of the community the friends develop the ability, willingness, courage and determination to obey the laws, apply the principles and administer the affairs of the Faith in accordance with divine precepts.

The new Plan revolves around a triple theme: enhancing the vitality of the faith of individual believers, greatly developing the human resources of the Cause, and fostering the proper functioning of local and national Bahá'í institutions. This is to lend focus to requisites of success as the Plan's manifold goals are pursued in these turbulent times....

Training of the friends and their striving, through serious individual study, to acquire knowledge of the Faith, to apply its principles and administer its affairs, are indispensable to developing the human resources necessary to the progress of the Cause. But knowledge alone is not adequate; it is vital that training be given in a manner that inspires love and devotion, fosters firmness in the Covenant, prompts the individual to active participation in the work of the Cause and to taking sound initiatives in the promotion of its interests. Special efforts to attract people of capacity to the Faith will also go far towards providing the human resources so greatly needed at this time. Moreover, these endeavours will stimulate and strengthen the ability of Spiritual Assemblies to meet their weighty responsibilities.

The proper functioning of these institutions depends largely on the efforts of their members to familiarize themselves with their duties and to adhere scrupulously to principle in their personal behaviour and in the conduct of their official responsibilities. Of relevant importance, too, are their resolve to remove all traces of estrangement and sectarian tendencies from their midst, their ability to win the affection and support of the friends under their care and to involve as many individuals as possible in the work of the Cause. By their constantly aiming at improving their performance, the communities they guide will reflect a pattern of life that will be a credit to the Faith and will, as a welcome consequence, rekindle hope among the increasingly disillusioned members of society.

(Riḍván 1993 message written by the Universal House of Justice to the Bahá'ís of the world)

49.   It is understandable that you feel concern about methods of teaching which apply pressure to people to declare their Faith in Bahá'u'lláh, or which register as believers those who apparently have no real knowledge of the Faith or its Message....

The teaching of the Cause has always called for wisdom, devotion, enthusiasm, purity of intention and eloquence of speech. Like other human beings, Bahá'ís tend to go to extremes, and too few people bring the proper balance to the way they act. This is particularly true in the teaching of the Faith. At one extreme are those who are so on fire with the love for the Faith and with awareness of the desperate need of the people for its healing Message, that they overstep the bounds of wisdom and discretion and stray into the area of proselytizing. At the other extreme are those who are so gentle in their approach and so concerned never to arouse an adverse reaction that they fail to convey the enormous importance of the Cause or to convince their hearers; for if the messenger is not enthusiastic, how can he convey enthusiasm to others? The first extreme leads to misrepresentation of the Teachings and causes disillusionment; the second results in the stagnation of the community and its failure to fulfil its fundamental duty of conveying this life-giving Message to the world.

In this, as in all aspects of the work of the Cause, the solution lies in the friends' being patient and forbearing towards those whose shortcomings distress them, and in endeavouring, through the Assemblies' consultation, to draw closer to a proper balance while maintaining the momentum of the work and canalizing the enthusiasm of the believers.

In one of its messages, published on page 32 of "Wellspring of Guidance", the Universal House of Justice gave the following advice:

Those who declare themselves as Bahá'ís should become enchanted with the beauty of the teachings, and touched by the love of Bahá'u'lláh. The declarants need not know all the proofs, history, laws, and principles of the Faith, but in the process of declaring themselves they must, in addition to catching the spark of faith, become basically informed about the Central Figures of the Faith, as well as the existence of laws they must follow and an administration they must obey.

In the western world in recent decades, Bahá'ís have grown used to thinking that the process by which a person accepts the Faith takes a long time, and that it is unthinkable for someone to intelligently accept Bahá'u'lláh within minutes of hearing of Him. This may be the pattern to which they have become accustomed, but it is far from being a universal one. When people accepted the Faith quickly in Africa and other parts of the Third World, western Bahá'ís sometimes explained it away by saying that such people were less educated and had fewer ideas to work their way through. Now the same process is happening in the countries of the former Eastern Bloc, and highly educated people are accepting the Faith as soon as they hear of it, embracing it enthusiastically, and rapidly deepening their understanding of its Teachings by reading every Bahá'í book they can lay their hands on. So it is clear that receptivity to spiritual truth is, as Bahá'u'lláh indicated, a matter of purity of heart, not of education or lack of it.

In the west of Europe, too, there are signs of greater receptivity towards the Faith among the people, and some are ready to join the community of the Most Great Name if approached in the proper manner. In such cases when an individual hears the Message of Bahá'u'lláh and is moved to declare his faith there should be no obstacle placed in his way. Great care must be taken that when the heart of the individual is touched by the power of Bahá'u'lláh's Message and the declarant has expressed his desire to embrace the Faith, the process of deepening be followed almost immediately. Deepening the knowledge of the new believer in the verities of the Faith is the most vital part of teaching; but deepening is not merely the imparting of knowledge — it requires also to imbue the soul of the person with the love of Bahá'u'lláh so that his faith may grow day by day and he becomes a steadfast believer.

In the following statement, Shoghi Effendi advises the Bahá'í teacher to advance the process of deepening for a person who is attracted to the Faith:

> Let him [the Bahá'í teacher] consider the degree of his hearer's receptivity, and decide for himself the suitability of either the direct or indirect method of teaching, whereby he can impress upon the seeker the vital importance of the Divine Message, and persuade him to throw in his lot with those who have already embraced it. Let him remember the example set by 'Abdu'l-Bahá, and His constant admonition to shower such kindness upon the seeker, and exemplify to such a degree the spirit of the teachings he hopes to instil into him,

that the recipient will be spontaneously impelled to identify himself with the Cause embodying such teachings. Let him refrain, at the outset, from insisting on such laws and observances as might impose too severe a strain on the seeker's newly awakened faith, and endeavour to nurse him, patiently, tactfully, and yet determinedly, into full maturity, and aid him to proclaim his unqualified acceptance of whatever has been ordained by Bahá'u'lláh. Let him, as soon as that stage has been attained, introduce him to the body of the fellow-believers, and seek, through constant fellowship and active participation in the local activities of his community, to enable him to contribute his share to the enrichment of its life, the furtherance of its tasks, the consolidations of its interests, and the coordination of its activities with those of its sister communities. Let him not be content until he has infused into his spiritual child so deep a longing as to impel him to arise independently, in his turn, and devote his energies to the quickening of other souls, and the upholding of the laws and principles laid down by his newly adopted Faith.

("The Advent of Divine Justice" (Wilmette: Bahá'í Publishing Trust, 1990), pp. 51-52)

From these words of the Guardian we can see that wisdom, encouragement, persuasion, and patience, are all called for, and that these must be attuned to the response shown by the hearer. We also see that the process of deepening continues long after the new believer has enrolled in the Bahá'í community.

(30 June 1993, written on behalf of the Universal House of Justice to an individual believer)

GUIDELINES FOR TEACHING

A Compilation Prepared by the Research Department of the Universal
House of Justice
Revised July 1990

The corner-stone of the foundation of all Bahá'í activity is teaching
the Cause. As 'Abdu'l-Bahá has categorically proclaimed in His Will
and Testament, "the guidance of the nations and peoples of the
world" is "the most important of things", and "Of all the gifts of God
the greatest is the gift of Teaching."

GUIDELINES FOR TEACHING

From the Writings of Bahá'u'lláh

50.   O Friends! You must all be so ablaze in this day with the fire of the love of God that the heat thereof may be manifest in all your veins, your limbs and members of your body, and the peoples of the world may be ignited by this heat and turn to the horizon of the Beloved.

(From a Tablet - translated from the Persian)

51.   Teach thou the Cause of God with an utterance which will cause the bushes to be enkindled, and the call 'Verily, there is no God but Me, the Almighty, the Unconstrained' to be raised therefrom. Say: Human utterance is an essence which aspireth to exert its influence and needeth moderation. As to its influence, this is conditional upon refinement which in turn is dependent upon hearts which are detached and pure. As to its moderation, this hath to be combined with tact and wisdom as prescribed in the Holy Scriptures and Tablets....

("Tablets of Bahá'u'lláh Revealed after the Kitáb-i-Aqdas", 1st pocket-sized ed. (Wilmette: Bahá'í Publishing Trust, 1988), p. 143)

52.   Moderation is indeed highly desirable. Every person who in some degree turneth towards the truth can himself later comprehend most of what he seeketh. However, if at the outset a word is uttered beyond his capacity, he will refuse to hear it and will arise in opposition.

(From a Tablet - translated from the Persian)

53.   ... Piety and detachment are even as two most great luminaries of the heaven of teaching. Blessed the one who hath attained unto this supreme station...

("Tablets of Bahá'u'lláh Revealed after the Kitáb-i-Aqdas", p. 253)

54.   Should any one among you be incapable of grasping a certain truth, or be striving to comprehend it, show forth, when conversing with him, a spirit of extreme kindliness and good-will. Help him to see and recognize the truth, without esteeming yourself to be, in the least, superior to him, or to be possessed of greater endowments.

The whole duty of man in this Day is to attain that share of the flood of grace which God poureth forth for him. Let none, therefore, consider the largeness or smallness of the receptacle. The portion of some might lie in the palm of a man's hand, the portion of others might fill a cup, and of others even a gallon-measure.

("Gleanings from the Writings of Bahá'u'lláh", rev. ed. (Wilmette: Bahá'í Publishing Trust, 1983), p. 8)

55. Consort with all men, O people of Bahá, in a spirit of friendliness and fellowship. If ye be aware of a certain truth, if ye possess a jewel, of which others are deprived, share it with them in a language of utmost kindliness and good-will. If it be accepted, if it fulfil its purpose, your object is attained. If any one should refuse it, leave him unto himself, and beseech God to guide him. Beware lest ye deal unkindly with him. A kindly tongue is the lodestone of the hearts of men. It is the bread of the spirit, it clotheth the words with meaning, it is the fountain of the light of wisdom and understanding....

("Gleanings from the Writings of Bahá'u'lláh", p. 289)

56. If he be kindled with the fire of His love, if he forgoeth all created things, the words he uttereth shall set on fire them that hear him.

(Cited in Shoghi Effendi, "The Advent of Divine Justice" (Wilmette: Bahá'í Publishing Trust, 1984), p. 51)

57. Say: O people of God! That which can insure the victory of Him Who is the Eternal Truth, His hosts and helpers on earth, have been set down in the sacred Books and Scriptures, and are as clear and manifest as the sun. These hosts are such righteous deeds, such conduct and character, as are acceptable in His sight. Whoso ariseth, in this Day, to aid Our Cause, and summoneth to his assistance the hosts of a praiseworthy character and upright conduct, the influence from such an action will, most certainly, be diffused throughout the whole world.

(Cited in Shoghi Effendi, "The Advent of Divine Justice", p. 24)

From the Writings of 'Abdu'l-Bahá

58.   Now is the time for you to divest yourselves of the garment of attachment to this world that perisheth, to be wholly severed from the physical world, become heavenly angels, and travel to these countries....

("Tablets of the Divine Plan Revealed by 'Abdu'l-Bahá to the North American Bahá'ís", rev. ed. (Wilmette: Bahá'í Publishing Trust, 1980), p. 34)

59.   With hearts overflowing with the love of God, with tongues commemorating the mention of God, with eyes turned to the Kingdom of God, they must deliver the Glad Tidings of the manifestation of the Lord of Hosts to all the people. Know ye of a certainty that whatever gathering ye enter, the waves of the Holy Spirit are surging over it, and the heavenly grace of the Blessed Beauty encompasseth that gathering.

("Tablets of the Divine Plan Revealed by 'Abdu'l-Bahá to the North American Bahá'ís", pp. 38-39)

60.   The aim is this: The intention of the teacher must be pure, his heart independent, his spirit attracted, his thought at peace, his resolution firm, his magnanimity exalted and in the love of God a shining torch. Should he become as such, his sanctified breath will even affect the rock; otherwise there will be no result whatsoever. As long as a soul is not perfected, how can he efface the defects of others. Unless he is detached from aught else save God, how can he teach severance to others!

("Tablets of the Divine Plan Revealed by 'Abdu'l-Bahá to the North American Bahá'ís", p. 51)

61.   ...rest ye assured in the confirmations of the Merciful and the assistances of the Most High; become ye sanctified above and purified from this world and the inhabitants thereof; suffer your intention to become for the good of all; cut your attachment to the earth and like unto the essence of the spirit become ye light and delicate. Then with a firm resolution, a pure heart, a rejoiced spirit, and an eloquent tongue, engage your time in the promulgation of the divine principles...

("Tablets of the Divine Plan Revealed by 'Abdu'l-Bahá to the North American Bahá'ís", p. 67)

62.   ...the believers of God must become self-sacrificing and like unto the candles of guidance become ignited... Should they show forth such a magnanimity, it is assured that they will obtain universal divine confirmations, the heavenly cohorts will reinforce them uninterruptedly, and a most great victory will be obtained....

("Tablets of the Divine Plan Revealed by 'Abdu'l-Bahá to the North American Bahá'ís", p. 27)

63.   O ye believers of God! Be not concerned with the smallness of your numbers, neither be oppressed by the multitude of an unbelieving world. Five grains of wheat will be endued with heavenly blessing, whereas a thousand tons of tares will yeild no results or effect. One fruitful tree will be conducive to the life of society, whereas a thousand forests of wild trees offer no fruits. The plain is covered with pebbles, but precious stones are rare. One pearl is better than a thousand wildernesses of sand, especially this pearl of great price, which is endowed with divine blessing. Ere long thousands of other pearls will be born from it. When that pearl associates and becomes the intimate of the pebbles, they also all change into pearls.

...rest ye not, seek ye no composure, attach not yourselves to the luxuries of this ephemeral world, free yourselves from every attachment, and strive with heart and soul to become fully established in the Kingdom of God. Gain ye the heavenly treasures. Day by day become ye more illumined. Draw ye nearer and nearer unto the threshold of oneness. Become ye the manifestors of spiritual favours and the dawning-places of infinite lights!...

As regards the teachers, they must completely divest themselves from the old garments and be invested with a new garment. According to the statement of Christ, they must attain to the station of rebirth — that is, whereas in the first instance they were born from the womb of the mother, this time they must be born from the womb of the world of nature. Just as they are now totally unaware of the experiences of the fetal world, they must also forget entirely the defects of the world of nature. They must be baptized with the water of life, the fire of the love of God and the breaths of the Holy Spirit; be satisfied with little food, but take a large portion from the heavenly table. They must disengage themselves from temptation and covetousness, and be filled with the spirit. Through the effect of their pure breath, they must change the stone into the brilliant ruby and the shell into pearl. Like unto the cloud of vernal shower, they must transform the black soil into the rose-garden and orchard. They must make the blind seeing, the deaf hearing, the extinguished one enkindled and set aglow, and the dead quickened.

("Tablets of the Divine Plan Revealed by 'Abdu'l-Bahá to the North American Bahá'ís", pp. 86-88)

64.   O thou maid-servant of God! Whenever thou art intending to deliver a speech, turn thy face toward the Kingdom of ABHA and, with a heart detached, begin to talk. The breaths of the Holy Spirit will assist thee.

("Tablets of Abdul-Baha Abbas", vol. 2 (Chicago: Bahá'í Publishing Committee, 1930 printing), p. 246)

65.   By the Lord of the Kingdom! If one arise to promote the Word of God with a pure heart, overflowing with the love of God and severed from the world, the Lord of Hosts will assist him with such a power as will penetrate the core of the existent beings.

("Tablets of Abdul-Baha Abbas", vol. 2, p. 348)

66.   Under all conditions the Message must be delivered, but with wisdom. If it be not possible openly, it must be done quietly. The friends should be engaged in educating the souls and should become instruments in aiding the world of humanity to acquire spiritual joy and fragrance. For example: If every one of the friends (believers) were to establish relations of friendship and right dealings with one of the negligent souls, associate and live with him with perfect kindliness, and meanwhile through good conduct and moral behaviour lead him to divine instruction, to heavenly advice and teachings, surely he would gradually arouse that negligent person and would change his ignorance into knowledge.

Souls are liable to estrangement. Such methods should be adopted that the estrangement should be first removed, then the Word will have effect.

If one of the believers be kind to one of the negligent ones and with perfect love should gradually make him understand the reality of the Cause of God in such a way that the latter should know in what manner the Religion of God hath been founded and what its object is, doubtless he will become changed; excepting abnormal souls who are reduced to the state of ashes and whose hearts are like stones, yea, even harder.

("Tablets of Abdul-Baha Abbas", vol. 2, p. 391)

67.   If thou wishest to guide the souls, it is incumbent on thee to be firm, to be good and to be imbued with praiseworthy attributes and divine qualities under all circumstances. Be a sign of love, a manifestation of mercy, a fountain of tenderness, kind-hearted, good to all and gentle to the servants of God, and especially to those who bear relation to thee, both men and women. Bear every ordeal that befalleth thee from the people and confront them not save with kindness, with great love and good wishes.

("Tablets of Abdul-Baha Abbas", vol. 3 (Chicago: Bahá'í Publishing Committee, 1930 printing), pp. 619-20)

68.   The teacher, when teaching, must be himself fully enkindled, so that his utterance, like unto a flame of fire, may exert influence and consume the veil of self and passion. He must also be utterly humble and lowly so that others may be edified, and be totally self-effaced and evanescent so that he may teach with the melody of the Concourse on high — otherwise his teaching will have no effect.

("Selections from the Writings of 'Abdu'l-Bahá", [rev. ed.] (Haifa: Bahá'í World Centre, 1982), Sec. 217, p. 270)

69.   When the friends do not endeavour to spread the message, they fail to remember God befittingly, and will not witness the tokens of assistance and confirmation from the Abhá Kingdom nor comprehend the divine mysteries. However, when the tongue of the teacher is engaged in teaching, he will naturally himself be stimulated, will become a magnet attracting the divine aid and bounty of the Kingdom, and will be like unto the bird at the hour of dawn, which itself becometh exhilarated by its own singing, its warbling and its melody.

("Selections from the Writings of 'Abdu'l-Bahá", Sec. 211, pp. 267-68)

70.   In accordance with the divine teachings in this glorious dispensation we should not belittle anyone and call him ignorant, saying: "You know not, but I know". Rather, we should look upon others with respect, and when attempting to explain and demonstrate, we should speak as if we are investigating the truth, saying: "Here these things are before us. Let us investigate to determine where and in what form the truth can be found." The teacher should not consider himself as learned and others ignorant. Such a thought breedeth pride, and pride is not conducive to influence. The teacher should not see in himself any superiority; he should speak with the utmost kindliness, lowliness and humility, for such speech exerteth influence and educateth the souls.

("Selections from the Writings of 'Abdu'l-Bahá", Sec. 15, p. 30)

71.   It is at such times that the friends of God avail themselves of the occasion, seize the opportunity, rush forth and win the prize. If their task is to be confined to good conduct and advice, nothing will be accomplished. They must speak out, expound the proofs, set forth clear arguments, draw irrefutable conclusions establishing the truth of the manifestation of the Sun of Reality.

("Selections from the Writings of 'Abdu'l-Bahá", Sec. 212, p. 268)

72.   When a speaker's brow shineth with the radiance of the love of God, at the time of his exposition of a subject, and he is exhilarated with the wine of true understanding, he becometh the centre of a potent force which like unto a magnet will attract the hearts. This is why the expounder must be in the utmost enkindlement.

(From a Tablet - translated from the Persian)

73.   Speak, therefore; speak out with great courage at every meeting. When you are about to begin your address, turn first to Bahá'u'lláh and ask for the confirmations of the Holy Spirit, then open your lips and say whatever is suggested to your heart; this, however, with the utmost courage, dignity and conviction....

("Selections from the Writings of 'Abdu'l-Bahá", Sec. 216 p. 269)

74.   As to his question about the permissibility of promulgating the divine teachings without relating them to the Most Great Name, you should answer: "This blessed Name hath an effect on the reality of things. If these teachings are spread without identifying them with this holy Name, they will fail to exert an abiding influence in the world. The teachings are like the body, and this holy Name is like the spirit. It imparteth life to the body. It causeth the people of the world to be aroused from their slumber."

(From a Tablet - translated from the Persian)

75.   The teaching work should under all conditions be actively pursued by the believers because divine confirmations are dependent upon it. Should a Bahá'í refrain from being fully, vigorously and wholeheartedly involved in the teaching work he will undoubtedly be deprived of the blessings of the Abhá Kingdom. Even so, this activity should be tempered with wisdom - not that wisdom which requireth one to be silent and forgetful of such an obligation, but rather that which requireth one to display divine tolerance, love, kindness, patience, a goodly character, and holy deeds. In brief, encourage the friends individually to teach the Cause of God and draw their attention to this meaning of wisdom mentioned in the Writings, which is itself the essence of teaching the Faith — but all this to be done with the greatest tolerance, so that heavenly assistance and divine confirmation may aid the friends.

("Selections from the Writings of 'Abdu'l-Bahá", Sec. 213, p. 268)

76.   The friends of God should weave bonds of fellowship with others and show absolute love and affection towards them. These links have a deep influence on people and they will listen. When the friends sense receptivity to the Word of God, they should deliver the Message with wisdom. They must first try and remove any apprehensions in the people they teach. In fact, every one of the believers should choose one person every year and try to establish ties of friendship with him, so that all his fear would disappear. Only then, and gradually, must he teach that person. This is the best method.

(From a Tablet - translated from the Persian)

77.   Follow thou the way of thy Lord, and say not that which the ears cannot bear to hear, for such speech is like luscious food given to small children. However palatable, rare and rich the food may be, it cannot be assimilated by the digestive organs of a suckling child. Therefore unto every one who hath a right, let his settled measure be given.

"Not everything that a man knoweth can be disclosed, nor can everything that he can disclose be regarded as timely, nor can every timely utterance be considered as suited to the capacity of those who hear it." Such is the consummate wisdom to be observed in thy pursuits. Be not oblivious thereof, if thou wishest to be a man of action under all conditions. First diagnose the disease and identify the malady, then prescribe the remedy, for such is the perfect method of the skilful physician.

("Selections from the Writings of 'Abdu'l-Bahá", Sec. 214, pp. 268-69)

78.   Do not argue with anyone, and be wary of disputation. Speak out the truth. If your hearer accepteth, the aim is achieved. If he is obdurate, you should leave him to himself, and place your trust in God. Such is the quality of those who are firm in the Covenant.

(From a Tablet - translated from the Persian)

79.   In this day every believer must concentrate his thoughts on teaching the Faith... O loved ones of God! Each one of the friends must teach at least one soul each year. This is everlasting glory. This is eternal grace.

(From a Tablet - translated from the Persian)

From the Writings of Shoghi Effendi and Letters Written on His Behalf

80.   First and foremost, one should use every possible means to purge one's heart and motives, otherwise, engaging in any form of enterprise would be futile. It is also essential to abstain from hypocrisy and blind imitation, inasmuch as their foul odour is soon detected by every man of understanding and wisdom. Moreover, the friends must observe the specific times for the remembrance of God, meditation, devotion and prayer, as it is highly unlikely, nay impossible, for any enterprise to prosper and develop when deprived of divine bestowals and confirmation. One can hardly imagine what a great influence genuine love, truthfulness and purity of motives exert on the souls of men. But these traits cannot be acquired by any believer unless he makes a daily effort to gain them....

It is primarily through the potency of noble deeds and character, rather than by the power of exposition and proofs, that the friends of God should demonstrate to the world that what has been promised by God is bound to happen, that it is already taking place and that the divine glad-tidings are clear, evident and complete....

(From a letter dated 19 December 1923 written by Shoghi Effendi to the Bahá'ís of the East - translated from the Persian)

81.   Having ... obtained a clear understanding of the true character of our mission, the methods to adopt, the course to pursue, and having attained sufficiently the individual regeneration — the essential requisite of teaching — let us arise to teach His Cause with righteousness, conviction,

understanding and vigour. Let this be the paramount and most urgent duty of every Bahá'í. Let us make it the dominating passion of our life. Let us scatter to the uttermost corners of the earth; sacrifice our personal interests, comforts, tastes and pleasures; mingle with the divers kindreds and peoples of the world; familiarize ourselves with their manners, traditions, thoughts and customs; arouse, stimulate and maintain universal interest in the Movement, and at the same time endeavour by all the means in our power, by concentrated and persistent attention, to enlist the unreserved allegiance and the active support of the more hopeful and receptive among our hearers. Let us too bear in mind the example which our beloved Master has clearly set before us. Wise and tactful in His approach, wakeful and attentive in His early intercourse, broad and liberal in all His public utterances, cautious and gradual in the unfolding of the essential verities of the Cause, passionate in His appeal yet sober in argument, confident in tone, unswerving in conviction, dignified in His manners — such were the distinguishing features of our Beloved's noble presentation of the Cause of Bahá'u'lláh.

("Bahá'í Administration: Selected Messages 1922-1932" [rev. ed.],
(Wilmette: Bahá'í Publishing Trust, 1980), pp. 69-70)

82.   Having on his own initiative, and undaunted by any hinderances with which either friend or foe may, unwittingly or deliberately, obstruct his path, resolved to arise and respond to the call of teaching, let him carefully consider every avenue of approach which he might utilize in his personal attempts to capture the attention, maintain the interest, and deepen the faith, of those whom he seeks to bring into the fold of his Faith. Let him survey the possibilities which the particular circumstances in which he lives offer him, evaluate their advantages, and proceed intelligently and systematically to utilize them for the achievement of the object he has in mind. Let him also attempt to devise such methods as association with clubs, exhibitions, and societies, lectures on subjects akin to the teachings and ideals of his Cause such as temperance, morality, social welfare, religious and racial tolerance, economic co-operation, Islám, and Comparative Religion, or participation in social, cultural, humanitarian, charitable, and educational organizations and enterprises which, while safeguarding the integrity of his Faith, will open up to him a multitude of ways and means whereby he can enlist successively the sympathy, the support, and ultimately the allegiance of those with whom he comes in contact. Let him, while such contacts are being made, bear in mind the claims which his Faith is constantly making upon him to preserve its dignity, and station, to safeguard the integrity of its laws and principles, to demonstate its comprehensiveness and universality, and to defend fearlessly its manifold and vital interests. Let him consider the degree of his hearer's receptivity, and decide for himself the suitability of either the direct or indirect method of teaching, whereby he can impress upon the seeker the vital importance of the Divine Message, and persuade him to throw in his lot with those who have already embraced it. Let him remember the example set by 'Abdu'l-Bahá, and His constant admonition to shower such kindness upon the seeker, and exemplify to such a degree the spirit of the teachings he hopes to instill into him, that the recipient will be spontaneously impelled to identify himself with the Cause embodying such teachings. Let him refrain, at the outset, from insisting on such laws and observances as might impose too severe a strain on the seeker's newly awakened faith, and endeavour to nurse him, patiently, tactfully, and yet determinedly, into full maturity, and aid him to proclaim his unqualified acceptance of whatever has been ordained by Bahá'u'lláh. Let him, as soon as that stage has been attained, introduce him to the body of his fellow-believers, and seek, through constant fellowship and active participation in the local activities of his community, to enable him to contribute his share to the enrichment of its life, the furtherance of its tasks, the consolidations of its interests, and the co-ordination of its activities with those if its sister communities. Let him not be content until he has infused into his spiritual child so deep a longing as to impel him to arise independently, in his turn, and devote his energies to the quickening of other souls, and the upholding of the laws and principles laid down by his newly adopted Faith.

("The Advent of Divine Justice", pp. 51-52)

83.   Every labourer in those fields, whether as traveling teacher or settler, should, I feel, make it his chief and constant concern to mix, in a friendly manner, with all sections of the population, irrespective of class, creed, nationality, or colour, to familiarize himself with their ideas, tastes, and habits, to study the approach best suited to them, to concentrate, patiently and tactfully, on a few who have shown marked capacity and receptivity, and to endeavour, with extreme kindness, to implant such love, zeal, and devotion in their hearts as to enable them to become in turn self-sufficient and independent promoters of the Faith in their respective localities....

("The Advent of Divine Justice", p. 65)

84.   Nor should any of the pioneers, at this early stage in the upbuilding of Bahá'í national communities, overlook the fundamental prerequisite for any successful teaching enterprise, which is to adapt the presentation of the fundamental principles of their Faith to the cultural and religious backgrounds, the ideologies, and the temperament of the divers races and nations whom they are called upon to enlighten and attract. The susceptibilities of these races and nations, from both the northern and southern climes, springing from either the Germanic or Latin stock, belonging to either the Catholic or Protestant communion, some democratic, others totalitarian in outlook, some socialistic, others capitalistic in their tendencies, differing widely in their customs and standards of living, should at all times be carefully considered, and under no circumstances neglected.

These pioneers, in their contact with the members of divers creeds, races and nations, covering a range which offers no parallel in either the north or south continents, must neither antagonize them nor compromise with their own essential principles. They must be neither provocative nor supine, neither fanatical nor excessively liberal, in their exposition of the fundamental and distinguishing features of their Faith. They must be either wary or bold, they must act swiftly or mark time, they must use the direct or indirect method, they must be challenging or conciliatory, in strict accordance with the spiritual receptivity of the soul with whom they come in contact, whether he be a nobleman or a commoner, a northerner or a southerner, a layman or a priest, a capitalist or a socialist, a statesman or a prince, an artisan or a beggar. In their presentation of the Message of Bahá'u'lláh they must neither hesitate nor falter. They must be neither comtemptuous of the poor nor timid before the great. In their exposition of its verities they must neither overstress nor whittle down the truth which they champion, whether their hearer belong to royalty, or be a prince of the church, or a politician, or a tradesman, or a man of the street. To all alike, high or low, rich or poor, they must proffer, with open hands, with a radiant heart, with an eloquent tongue, with infinite patience, with uncompromising loyalty, with great wisdom, with unshakable courage, the Cup of Salvation at so critical an hour, to the confused, the hungry, the distraught and fear-stricken multitudes, in the north, in the west, in the south and in the heart, of that sorely tried continent.

("Citadel of Faith: Messages to America 1947-1957" (Wilmette: Bahá'í Publishing Trust, 1980), pp. 25-26)

85.   The individual alone must assess its character, consult his conscience, prayerfully consider all its aspects, manfully struggle against the natural inertia that weighs him down in his effort to arise, shed, heroically and irrevocably, the trivial and superfluous attachments which hold him back, empty himself of every thought that may tend to obstruct his path, mix, in obedience to the counsels of the Author of His Faith, and in imitation of the One Who is its true Exemplar, with men and women, in all walks of life, seek to touch their hearts, through the distinction which characterizes his thoughts, his words and his acts, and win them over tactfully, lovingly, prayerfully and persistently, to the Faith he himself has espoused.

("Citadel of Faith: Messages to America 1947-1957", p. 148)

86.   ...revisit all the centres where you have already sown the seed, in order to water the seedlings that have taken root and to sow fresh good seed in the prepared ground.

(From a letter dated 9 April 1925 written on behalf of Shoghi Effendi to two believers)

87.   Entire and selfless devotion is what is most needful. The brighter our torch burns, the more light will it give and the more readily will it impart its blaze to others....

(From a letter dated 3 May 1925 written on behalf of Shoghi Effendi to an individual believer)

88.   Shoghi Effendi feels that he can lay down no rule as to when one should introduce the names of the Báb, Bahá'u'lláh and 'Abdu'l-Bahá in one's teaching. Much depends on the temperament and aptitude both of the teacher and the one taught....

...

We must look to the example of the Master and follow our "Inner Light", adapting our message as best we can to the capacity and "ripeness" of the one we are seeking to teach....

Man's spiritual digestive powers have similar laws to those that govern physical digestion. When people are spiritually hungry and thirsty they must be given wholesome and suitable spiritual food, but if we give too much at a time or too rich food for the digestive powers, it only causes nausea and rejection or malassimilation.

(From a letter dated 20 October 1925 written on behalf of Shoghi Effendi to two believers)

89.   Although teaching the Cause is the duty of every real Bahá'í and must be our main aim in life, to obtain the best results extensive and organized efforts at teaching must be by the approval and through the help and supervision of either the Local or the National Spiritual Assemblies. Shoghi Effendi hopes that you will translate your earnestness and enthusiasm into real service in close co-operation with the friends and the Assemblies.

(From a letter dated 31 May 1926 written on behalf of Shoghi Effendi to an individual believer)

90.   In spreading the Cause we should be mindful not to lower its prestige and also try and get the people whom we approach really attracted. Shoghi Effendi has often in his letters mentioned the importance of follow-up work. Seeds sown but not watered and reared will not mature into fruition.

(From a letter dated 13 August 1928 written on behalf of Shoghi Effendi to an individual believer)

91.   Perhaps the reason why you have not accomplished so much in the field of teaching is the extent you looked upon your own weaknesses and inabilities to spread the message. Bahá'u'lláh and the Master have both urged us repeatedly to disregard our own handicaps and lay our whole reliance upon God. He will come to our help if we only arise and become an active channel for God's grace. Do you think it is the teachers who make converts and change human hearts? No, surely not. They are only pure souls who take the first step, and then let the spirit of Bahá'u'lláh move them and make use of them. If any one of them should even for a second consider his achievements as due to his own capacities, his work is ended and his fall starts. This is in fact the reason why so many competent souls have after wonderful services suddenly found themselves absolutely impotent and perhaps thrown aside by the Spirit of the Cause as useless souls. The criterion is the extent to which we are ready to have the will of God operate through us.

Stop being conscious of your frailties, therefore; have a perfect reliance upon God; let your heart burn with the desire to serve His mission and proclaim His call; and you will observe how eloquence and the power to change human hearts will come as a matter of course.

Shoghi Effendi will surely pray for your success if you should arise and start to teach. In fact the mere act of arising will win for you God's help and blessings.

(From a letter dated 31 March 1932 written on behalf of Shoghi Effendi to an individual believer)

92. It is on young and active Bahá'ís, like you, that the Guardian centres all his hopes for the future progress and expansion of the Cause, and it is on their shoulders that he lays all the responsibility for the upkeep of the spirit of selfless service among their fellow-believers. Without that spirit no work can be successfully achieved. With it triumph, though hardly won, is but inevitable. You should, therefore, try all your best to carry aflame within you the torch of faith, for through it you will surely find guidance, strength and eventual success.

...every one of them is able, in his own measure, to deliver the Message ... Everyone is a potential teacher. He has only to use what God has given him and thus prove that he is faithful to his trust.

(From a letter dated 1 September 1933 written on behalf of Shoghi Effendi to an individual believer)

93. In teaching the Cause, much depends on the personality of the teacher and on the method he chooses for presenting the message. Different personalities and different classes and types of individuals need different methods of approach. And it is the sign of an able teacher to know how to best adapt his methods to various types of people whom he happens to meet. There is no one method one can follow all through. But there should be as many ways of approach as there are types of individual seekers. Flexibility and variety of method is, therefore, an essential prerequisite for the success of every teaching activity.

(From a letter dated 31 May 1934 written on behalf of Shoghi Effendi to an individual believer)

94. There are innumerable ways of teaching the Cause. You can choose the one that suits best your nature and capacity.

(From a letter dated 13 November 1935 written on behalf of Shoghi Effendi to an individual believer)

95.   A true and adequate knowledge of the Cause is, indeed, indispensable to every one who wishes to successfully teach the Message. The book of "Gleanings" gives the friends a splendid opportunity to acquire this necessary knowledge and understanding. It gives them, in addition, that inspiration and spiritual fervour which the reading of the Holy Words can alone impart.
(From a letter dated 2 December 1935 written on behalf of Shoghi Effendi to an individual believer)

96.   What the Guardian feels it of vital importance for the friends to do is to teach the Cause directly and by means of imparting the Holy Words....
(From a letter dated 6 May 1936 written on behalf of Shoghi Effendi to an individual believer)

97.   It is in intellectual circles such as this that the believers should endeavour to teach, confident that no matter how limited their capacity may be, yet their efforts are continually guided and reinforced from on High. This spirit of confident hope, of cheerful courage, and of undaunted enthusiasm in itself, irrespective of any tangible results which it may procure, can alone ensure the ultimate success of our teaching efforts.
(From a letter dated 31 October 1936 written on behalf of Shoghi Effendi to an individual believer)

98.   ...the upper classes ... need the right type of people to approach them, and a method that can suit their mentality. Our teaching methods should allow a certain degree of elasticity in establishing contacts with various types of individual seekers. Every inquirer has to be approached from his own angle. Those who are essentially of the mystic type should first be given those teachings of the Cause which emphasize the nature and value of spiritual realities; while those who are practically minded and of a positive type are naturally more ready and inclined to accept the social aspect of the Teachings. But of course, gradually the *entire* Message, in all its aspects and with the full implications it entails, should be explained to the newcomer. For to be a believer means to accept the Cause in its wholeness, and not to adhere to some of its teachings. However, as already stated, this ought to be done gradually and tactfully. For conversion is after all a slow process.
(From a letter dated 28 December 1936 written on behalf of Shoghi Effendi to an individual believer)

99. Do not feel discourag[ed] if your labours do not always yield an abundant fruitage. For a quick and rapidly-won success is not always the best and the most lasting. The harder you strive to attain your goal, the greater will be the confirmations of Bahá'u'lláh, and the more certain you can feel to attain success. Be cheerful, therefore, and exert yourself with full faith and confidence. For Bahá'u'lláh has promised His Divine assistance to everyone who arises with a pure and detached heart to spread His holy Word, even though he may be bereft of every human knowledge and capacity, and notwithstanding the forces of darkness and of opposition which may be arrayed against him. The goal is clear, the path safe and certain, and the assurances of Bahá'u'lláh as to the eventual success of our efforts quite emphatic. Let us keep firm, and whole-heartedly carry on the great work which He has entrusted into our hands.

(From a letter dated 3 February 1937 written on behalf of Shoghi Effendi to an individual believer)

100. The Bahá'í teacher must be all confidence. Therein lies his strength and the secret of his success. Though single-handed, and no matter how great the apathy of the people around you may be, you should have faith that the hosts of the Kingdom are on your side, and that through their help you are bound to overcome the forces of darkness that are facing the Cause of God. Persevere, be happy and confident, therefore.

(From a letter dated 30 June 1937 written on behalf of Shoghi Effendi to an individual believer)

101. ...refrain, under any circumstances, from involving yourselves, much less the Cause, in lengthy discussions of a controversial character, as these besides being fruitless actually cause incalculable harm to the Faith. Bahá'u'lláh has repeatedly urged us not to engage in religious controversies, as the adepts of former religions have done. The Bahá'í teacher should be concerned above all in presenting the Message, in explaining and clarifying all its aspects, rather than in attacking other religions. He should avoid all situations that, he feels, would lead to strife, to hair-splitting and interminable discussions.

(From a letter dated 29 November 1937 written on behalf of Shoghi Effendi to an individual believer)

102.   The believers ought to give the Message even to those who do not seem to be ready for it, because they can never judge the real extent to which the Word of God can influence the hearts and minds of the people, even those who appear to lack any power of receptivity to the Teachings.
(From a letter dated 14 January 1938 written on behalf of Shoghi Effendi to an individual believer)

103.   The love we bear mankind, our conviction that Bahá'u'lláh's Faith contains the only and the Divine remedy for all its ills, must be demonstrated today in action by bringing the Cause before the public. No doubt the majority are not yet able to see its true significance, but they must not be deprived, through our failure in obligation, of the opportunity of hearing of it. And there are many precious souls who are seeking for it and ready to embrace it.
(From a letter dated 19 March 1942 written on behalf of Shoghi Effendi to an individual believer)

104.   If the friends always waited until they were fully qualified to do any particular task, the work of the Cause would be almost at a standstill! But the very act of striving to serve, however unworthy one may feel, attracts the blessings of God and enables one to become more fitted for the task.

Today the need is so great on the part of humanity to hear of the Divine Message, that the believers must plunge into the work, wherever and however they can, heedless of their own shortcomings, but ever heedful of the crying need of their fellow-men to hear of the teachings in their darkest hour of travail.
(From a letter dated 4 May 1942 written on behalf of Shoghi Effendi to an individual believer)

105.   The Cause of God has room for all. It would, indeed, not be the Cause of God if it did not take in and welcome everyone — poor and rich, educated and ignorant, the unknown, and the prominent — God surely wants them all, as He created them all.
(From a letter dated 10 December 1942 written on behalf of Shoghi Effendi to two believers)

106.   ...no system, for teachers to practise, exists. But obviously the more people know about the teachings and the Cause, the better they will be able to present the subject. If some people find that prayer and placing all their trust in God, releases in them a flood of inspiration, they should be left free to pursue this method if it is productive of results.

(From a letter dated 25 January 1943 written on behalf of Shoghi Effendi to two believers)

107.   Through example, loving fellowship, prayer, and kindness the friends can attract the hearts of such people and enable them to realize that this is the Cause of God in deed, not merely words!...

(From a letter dated 24 February 1943 written on behalf of Shoghi Effendi to an individual believer)

108.   Unless and until the believers really come to realize they are one spiritual family, knit together by a bond more lasting than mere physical ties can ever be, they will not be able to create that warm community atmosphere which alone can attract the hearts of humanity, frozen for lack of real love and feeling.

(From a letter dated 5 May 1943 written on behalf of Shoghi Effendi to an individual believer)

109.   Not all of us are capable of serving in the same way, but the one way every Bahá'í can spread the Faith is by example. This moves the hearts of people far more deeply than words ever can.

The love we show others, the hospitality and understanding, the willingness to help them, these are the very best advertisements of the Faith....

(From a letter dated 14 October 1943 written on behalf of Shoghi Effendi to an individual believer)

110.   By all means persevere and associate in a friendly spirit with other groups of young people, particularly of a different race or minority nationality, for such association will demonstrate your complete conviction of the oneness of mankind and attract others to the Faith, both young and old alike.

A spirit of prejudice-free, loving comradeship with others is what will open the eyes of people more than any amount of words. Combined with such deeds you can teach the Faith easily.

(From a letter dated 18 June 1945 written on behalf of Shoghi Effendi to the Bahá'ís of Dayton, Oh)

111.   ...a sound knowledge of history, including religious history, and also of social and economic subjects, is of great help in teaching the Cause to intelligent people...

(From a letter dated 4 May 1946 written on behalf of Shoghi Effendi to an individual believer)

112.   He feels you should, in teaching, certainly not start with such a difficult point as abstinence from wine; but when the person wishes to join the Faith he must be told....

(From a letter dated 7 April 1947 written on behalf of Shoghi Effendi to two believers)

113.   All the Bahá'ís, new and old alike, should devote themselves as much as possible to teaching the Faith; they should also realize that the atmosphere of true love and unity which they manifest within the Bahá'í Community will directly affect the public, and be the greatest magnet for attracting people to the Faith and confirming them.

(From a letter dated 4 April 1947 written on behalf of Shoghi Effendi to the Local Spiritual Assembly of Stuttgart, Germany)

114.   In teaching people, when they begin to seriously study the Faith there is no objection to impressing upon them that this message involves great spiritual responsibility, and should not be either accepted or cast aside lightly. But we must be very gentle, tactful and patient, and not administer shocks to people.

We must always teach constructively, and be very sure that none of us, through disagreement among ourselves or indiscretion, cool off the souls of the seekers.

(From a letter dated 14 October 1947 written on behalf of Shoghi Effendi to an individual believer)

115.   There is no objection to leaving Bahá'í Literature in a public place as long as it is not overdone and does not savour of proselytizing.

(From a letter dated 22 December 1947 written on behalf of Shoghi Effendi to an individual believer)

116.   ...it is spirit, determination, faith and devotion which bring victories into being, one after another, in Britain, and not luxury and leisure....

(From a letter dated 29 April 1948 written on behalf of Shoghi Effendi to the National Spiritual Assembly of the British Isles)

117.   We should never insist on teaching those who are not really ready for the Cause. If a man is not hungry you cannot make him eat. Among the Theosophists there are, no doubt, many receptive souls, but those who are satisfied should be just associated with in a friendly way, but let alone. Once a seeker comes to accept the concept of progressive religion, and accepts Bahá'u'lláh as the Manifestation for this day, the reincarnation concept will fade away in the light of truth; we should try and avoid controversial issues in the beginning, if possible.

(From a letter dated 23 June 1948 written on behalf of Shoghi Effendi to an individual believer)

118.   It seems what we need now is a more profound and co-ordinated Bahá'í scholarship in order to attract such men as you are contacting. The world has — at least the thinking world — caught up by now with all the great and universal principles enunciated by Bahá'u'lláh over 70 years ago, and so of course it does not sound "new" to them. But we know that the deeper teachings, the capacity of His projected World Order to re-create society, are new and dynamic. It is these we must learn to present intelligently and enticingly to such men!

(From a letter dated 3 July 1949 written on behalf of Shoghi Effendi to an individual believer)

119.   ...we, the few who have caught the vision, should not waste our energies beating up and down the paths pursued by humanity, and which are not solving its ghastly present-day problems. We should concentrate on the Cause, because it is what is needed to cure the world....

If the Bahá'ís want to be really effective in teaching the Cause they need to be much better informed and able to discuss intelligently, intellectually, the present condition of the world and its problems....

We Bahá'ís should, in other words, arm our minds with knowledge in order to better demonstrate to, especially, the educated classes, the truths enshrined in our Faith....

(From a letter dated 5 July 1949 written on behalf of Shoghi Effendi to an individual believer)

120.   Teaching individually is of great importance, and often enables you to confirm people, whereas public speaking, while it carries the Message to more people, does not confirm very many. You can do both.

(From a letter dated 5 August 1949 written on behalf of Shoghi Effendi to an individual believer)

121.   ...when we put our trust in Him, Bahá'u'lláh solves our problems and opens the way.

(From a letter dated 12 October 1949 written on behalf of Shoghi Effendi to an individual believer)

122.   To find these receptive souls and teach them, with tact and understanding, is the duty and privilege of every single Bahá'í.

(From a letter dated 20 October 1949 written on behalf of Shoghi Effendi to an individual believer)

123.   Without the spirit of real love for Bahá'u'lláh, for His Faith and its Institutions, and the believers for each other, the Cause can never really bring in large numbers of people. For it is not preaching and rules the world wants, but love and action.

(From a letter dated 25 October 1949 written on behalf of Shoghi Effendi to an individual believer)

124.   Just one mature soul, with spiritual understanding and a profound knowledge of the Faith, can set a whole country ablaze — so great is the power of the Cause to work through a pure and selfless channel.

(From a letter dated 6 November 1949 written on behalf of Shoghi Effendi to an individual believer)

125.   As we have such wonderful prayers and meditations in our writings, the reading of these with friends who are interested in and crave for this type of small meeting is often a step towards attracting them to the Faith. Perhaps you could start such an activity in your city.

(From a letter dated 4 February 1950 written on behalf of Shoghi Effendi to an individual believer)

126. The believers are entirely free to hold as many little teaching groups or Firesides as they please in their own homes... In fact this personal, informal, home teaching is perhaps the most productive of results.
(From a letter dated 24 February 1950 written on behalf of Shoghi Effendi to an individual believer)

127. ...make a special point of praying ardently not only for success in general, but that God may send to you the souls that are ready. There are such souls in every city...
(From a letter dated 18 March 1950 written on behalf of Shoghi Effendi to the Local Spiritual Assembly of Punta Arenas)

128. The people of the world are submerged in an atmosphere which is the very antithesis, morally, of the Bahá'í atmosphere; we must teach them. If we are too strict in the beginning most — not all — types will be rebuffed and veer away from what they might otherwise be led to accept. On the other hand, we don't want Bahá'ís who do not seriously try to live up to the teachings — we must therefore use great tact and challenge strong souls and lead weak souls.
(From a letter dated 7 August 1950 written on behalf of Shoghi Effendi to an individual believer)

129. At all times we must look at the greatness of the Cause, and remember that Bahá'u'lláh will assist all who arise in His service. When we look at ourselves, we are sure to feel discouraged by our shortcomings and insignificance!
(From a letter dated 12 December 1950 written on behalf of Shoghi Effendi to an individual believer)

130. The excellent work you are doing in the teaching field, he appreciates very deeply and wishes you to persevere and go on teaching people of importance. Even if they are not always good prospects as far as being converted to the Faith goes, it is very necessary that they should hear of it and be made friendly towards it.

(From a letter dated 10 February 1951 written on behalf of Shoghi Effendi to an individual believer)

131. Although it is good not to provoke conventional people too much, on the other hand, we must not allow them to come between us and obeying Bahá'u'lláh; and we know that He has instructed His servants to spread His Message....

(From a letter dated 1 May 1951 written on behalf of Shoghi Effendi to an individual believer)

132. ...whilst actively teaching, the friends must themselves be taught and deepened in the spirit of the Faith, which brings love and unity.

(From a letter dated 17 July 1951 written on behalf of Shoghi Effendi to an individual believer)

133. These people, finding the Bahá'ís *sincerely* lacking in either prejudice — or that even worse attitude, condescension — might not only take interest in our Teachings, but also help us to reach their people in the proper way.

It is a great mistake to believe that because people are illiterate or live primitive lives, they are lacking in either intelligence or sensibility. On the contrary, they may well look on us, with the evils of our civilization, with its moral corruption, its ruinous wars, its hypocrisy and conceit, as people who merit watching with both suspicion and contempt. We should meet them as equals, well-wishers, people who admire and respect their ancient descent, and who feel that they will be interested, as we are, in a living religion and not in the dead forms of present-day churches.

(From a letter dated 21 September 1951 written on behalf of Shoghi Effendi to the National Teaching Committee of the National Spiritual Assembly of Argentina, Chile, Uruguay, Paraguay and Bolivia)

134. Teaching is of course the head corner-stone of all Bahá'í service, but successful teaching is dependent upon many factors, one of which is the development of a true Bahá'í way of living and the fulfilment of responsibilities which we have incurred.

(From a letter dated 3 June 1952 written on behalf of Shoghi Effendi to an individual believer)

135.   It should not be overlooked, however, that the most powerful and effective teaching medium that has been found so far is the fireside meeting, because in the fireside meeting, intimate personal questions can be answered, and the student find the spirit of the Faith more abundant there.

(From a letter dated 11 December 1952 written on behalf of Shoghi Effendi to a Local Spiritual Assembly and an individual believer)

136.   Today, as never before, the magnet which attracts the blessings from on high is teaching the Faith of God. The Hosts of Heaven are poised between heaven and earth, just waiting, and patiently, for the Bahá'í to step forth, with pure devotion and consecration, to teach the Cause of God, so they may rush to his aid and assistance. It is the Guardian's prayer that the Friends may treble their efforts, as the time is short — alas, the workers too few. Let those who wish to achieve immortality step forth and raise the Divine Call. They will be astonished at the spiritual victories they will gain.

(From a letter dated 28 March 1953 written on behalf of Shoghi Effendi to an individual believer)

137.   What is needed to achieve success in the teaching field is a complete dedication on the part of the individual, consecration to the glorious task of spreading the Faith, and the living of the Bahá'í life, because that creates the magnet for the Holy Spirit, and it is the Holy Spirit which quickens the new soul. Thus the individual should be as a reed, through which the Holy Spirit may flow, to give new life to the seeking soul.

One should search out those who are receptive to the Faith, and then concentrate on these persons in their teaching.

(From a letter dated 18 December 1953 written on behalf of Shoghi Effendi to an individual believer)

138.   The peoples generally are seeking the light of Divine Guidance. The problems of the world have awakened the populace. It only remains for the Bahá'ís to raise the Call and give the Message according to the high standards enunciated by the beloved Master. The world can become alive with the gifts of the Holy Spirit, if the Bahá'ís fulfil their sacred obligation.

In pioneering fields, and on the home front, the friends must arise with the same spirit of dedication and consecration which animated the original pioneers. If they do, they will be astonished at the great results they will achieve.

...

Setting aside all the shibboleths of present-day living, leaving behind the false standards of those endeavouring to solve the world's problems by weak platitudes, and demonstrating the new Bahá'í way of dynamic spiritual living, let them, relying on the guidance of the Holy Spirit, arise to spread the Water of Life over America. This will produce the results which the cries of humanity today require. Where are the spiritual souls who will now seize their opportunity, and achieve immortal glory in the service of the Faith!

(From a letter dated 14 April 1954 written on behalf of Shoghi Effendi to the National Spiritual Assembly of the United States)

139.   As you interest different ones in the Faith, you must be very cautious, and gradually lead them into the Light of Divine Guidance, especially the practices of Bahá'í living. Thus you should not be dogmatic about any of the secondary practices of the Faith....

(From a letter dated 5 June 1954 written on behalf of Shoghi Effendi to an individual believer)

140.   The Guardian feels that the most effective way for the Bahá'ís to teach the Faith is to make strong friends with their neighbours and associates. When the friends have confidence in the Bahá'ís and the Bahá'ís in their friends, they should give the Message and teach the Cause. Individual teaching of this type is more effective than any other type.

The principle of the fireside meeting, which was established in order to permit and encourage the individual to teach in his own home, has been proven the most effective instrument for spreading the Faith....

(From a letter dated 27 December 1954 written on behalf of Shoghi Effendi to an individual believer)

141.   It is better to have one Bahá'í who understands the Teachings and is wholeheartedly convinced of their truth, than a number of Bahá'ís, who are not well aware of the Cause, and deep-rooted in the Covenant.

(From a letter dated 22 January 1955 written on behalf of Shoghi Effendi to an individual believer)

142. Consecration, dedication and enthusiastic service is the Keynote to successful teaching. One must become like a reed through which the Holy Spirit descends to reach the student of the Faith.

We give the Message, and explain the Teachings, but it is the Holy Spirit that quickens and confirms.

(From a letter dated 16 February 1955 written on behalf of Shoghi Effendi to an individual believer)

143. The Guardian thinks perhaps a different approach to the aborigines might attract them; one of being interested in their lives and their folklore, and of trying to become their friend, rather than trying to change them or improve them.

(From a letter dated 9 April 1955 written on behalf of Shoghi Effendi to an individual believer)

144. The Bahá'ís must realize that the success of this work depends upon the individual. The individual must arise as never before to proclaim the Faith of Bahá'u'lláh. The most effective way for them to carry on their work is for the individual to make many contacts, select a few who they feel would become Bahá'ís, develop a close friendship with them, then complete confidence, and finally teach them the Faith, until they become strong supporters of the Cause of God.

(From a letter dated 13 May 1955 written on behalf of Shoghi Effendi to all National Spiritual Assemblies)

145. The all-important thing of course is that every activity ... is for the purpose of teaching the Faith and confirming people. Therefore you and the other Bahá'ís should watch the situation very closely. You should study those who attend the meetings, and when you find one who you feel would become a strong and active Bahá'í, then you should concentrate on teaching him. Thus, if you are able to confirm some souls, you will have rendered distinguished and outstanding service. Actually this is the goal of all such activities in all of the universities.

(From a letter dated 1 June 1955 written on behalf of Shoghi Effendi to an individual believer)

146.   The Hosts of the Supreme Concourse are in martial array, poised between Earth and Heaven ready to rush to the assistance of those who arise to Teach the Faith. If one seeks the confirmation of the Holy Spirit, one can find it in rich abundance in the Teaching Field. The world is seeking as never before, and if the Friends will arise with new determination, fully consecrated to the noble task ahead of them, victory after victory will be won for the Glorious Faith of God.

(From a letter dated 2 February 1956 written on behalf of Shoghi Effendi to an individual believer)

147.   The greatest glory and honour which can come to an individual is to bring the light of guidance to some new soul. The quickening power of the Holy Spirit, which has come into the world through Bahá'u'lláh, is the source of immortal life; and those who are quickened by this spirit in this world will find themselves in great honour and glory in the next world. The most meritorious service which anyone could render is to bring the light of divine guidance and the quickening power of the spirit to an entirely new area. Humanity is crying for salvation; and it is only by the Bahá'ís going into the various areas of the world, that it can be brought to them. This is the reason the Guardian has encouraged all of the friends to disperse to new territories, for this is the hour for the quickening of the world.

(From a letter dated 11 March 1956 written on behalf of Shoghi Effendi to the Bahá'í Community of Tacoma, US)

148.   The need of the Hour is Teaching on the Home Front. Its goals can be won, by a new spirit of dedication and consecration on the part of the friends, each in his own country, in his own home.... Never must they let a day pass without teaching some soul, trusting to Bahá'u'lláh that the seed will grow. The friends should seek pure souls, gain their confidence, and then teach that person carefully until he becomes a Bahá'í, and then nurture him until he becomes a firm and active supporter of the Faith.

Everyone must remember that it is the "Holy Spirit that quickens" and therefore the teacher must become like a reed through which the Holy Spirit may reach the seeking soul.

The beloved Guardian has stressed over and over again, that to effectively teach the Faith, the individual must *study* deeply, the Divine Word, imbibe Its life-giving waters, and feast upon Its glorious teachings. He should then *meditate* on the import of the Word, and finding its spiritual depths, *pray* for guidance and assistance. But most important, after prayer is *action.* After one has prayed and meditated, he must arise, relying fully on the guidance and confirmation of Bahá'u'lláh, to teach His Faith. *Perseverance* in action is essential, just as wisdom and audacity are necessary for effective teaching. The individual must sacrifice all things to this great goal, and then the victories will be won.

(From a letter dated 30 May 1956 written on behalf of Shoghi Effendi to the Hands of the Cause in the United States)

149.   The spirit of the hour is teaching on the Home Fronts. Its goal can only be won by a new spirit of dedication and consecration on the part of the friends at home. Miraculous victories are being won, in the difficult virgin areas, because the pioneers have consecrated their lives to the Noble Mission they have embarked upon. The Friends at home must display this same consecration and dedication. Never must they let a day pass, without teaching some soul, hoping that Bahá'u'lláh will cause each seed to grow. The Friends should seek pure souls, gain their confidence and then teach that person carefully until he becomes a Bahá'í — and then nurture him until he becomes a firm and active supporter of the Faith.

(From a letter dated 15 June 1956 written on behalf of Shoghi Effendi to the Bahá'ís of Lafayette, In)

150.   He hopes you will be guided and confirmed in your work, so many souls may find eternal life, through your selfless services. It is important that you make contact with pure hearted individuals, gain their confidence, they gain confidence in you, and then gradually teach them. It is better to concentrate on a few, rather than attempt to teach too many at a time. Consecration, devotion, dedication, humility are essential, that the Holy Spirit may use you as a reed for the diffusion of Its creative rays.

(From a letter dated 15 July 1956 written on behalf of Shoghi Effendi to an individual believer)

151.   The Guardian feels that, if the friends would meditate a little more objectively upon both their relationship to the Cause and the vast non-Bahá'í public they hope to influence, they would see things more clearly.... He fully realizes that the demands made upon the Bahá'ís are great, and that they often feel inadequate, tired and perhaps frightened in the face of the tasks that confront them. This is only natural. On the other hand, they must realize that the power of God can and will assist them; and that because they are privileged to have accepted the Manifestation of God for this Day, this very act has placed upon them a great moral responsibility toward their fellow-men. It is this moral responsibility to which the Guardian is constantly calling their attention...

(From a letter dated 19 July 1956 written on behalf of Shoghi Effendi to the National Spiritual Assembly of the United States)

152. The friends must certainly explore new channels and have more audacity, if they are to get anywhere in adding to their numbers.

(From a letter dated 6 October 1956 written on behalf of Shoghi Effendi to an individual believer)

153. The most effective method of teaching is the Fireside group, where new people can be shown Bahá'í hospitality, and ask all questions which bother them. They can feel there the true Bahá'í spirit — and it is the spirit that quickeneth.

(From a letter dated 20 October 1956 written on behalf of Shoghi Effendi to an individual believer)

154. He feels that to distribute Bahá'í pamphlets from door to door ... is undignified and might create a bad impression of the Faith....

(From a letter dated 20 October 1956 written on behalf of Shoghi Effendi to the National Spiritual Assembly of Canada)

155. We must be careful not to teach in a fanatical way. We should teach as the Master taught. He was the perfect Exemplar of the Teachings. He proclaimed the universal truths, and, through love and wise demonstration of the universal verities of the Faith, attracted the hearts and the minds.

(From a letter dated 20 October 1956 written on behalf of Shoghi Effendi to an individual believer)

156. The Master assured us that when we forget ourselves, and strive with all our powers to serve and teach the Faith, we receive divine assistance. It is not we who do the work, but we are the instruments used at that time for the purpose of teaching His Cause.

(From a letter dated 8 November 1956 written on behalf of Shoghi Effendi to an individual believer)

157.   The Teaching of the Faith is dependent on the individual and his effort. When the individual arises with enthusiasm, with full dedication and consecration, and allows nothing to deter him; then results will be achieved....

(From a letter dated 17 December 1956 written on behalf of Shoghi Effendi to the Bahá'ís assembled at the Indiana State Convention)

158.   The Guardian hopes the Friends ... will display the loving spirit of the Master in their contacts, and then win those souls to the Faith. The fireside method of teaching seems to produce the greatest results, when each one invites friends into their homes once in nineteen days, and introduces them to the Faith. Close association and loving service affects the hearts; and when the heart is affected, then the spirit can enter. It is the Holy Spirit that quickens, and the Friends must become channels for its diffusion.

(From a letter dated 27 January 1957 written on behalf of Shoghi Effendi to an individual believer)

159.   The Guardian was very happy to receive the news of the sudden spurt in the number of Friends joining the Faith. It demonstrates that one must persevere until the very end, if success is to be achieved....

(From a letter dated 19 April 1957 written on behalf of Shoghi Effendi to an individual believer)

160.   ...the world is being shaken to its foundations and the people are seeking. If the Bahá'ís will arise as never before to teach the Cause they will find many listeners and many will find eternal life through their sacrificial efforts.

(From a letter dated 17 May 1957 written on behalf of Shoghi Effendi to the National Spiritual Assembly of Canada)

161.   Divine Truth is relative and that is why we are enjoined to constantly refer the seeker to the Word itself — and why any explanations we make to ease the journey of the soul of any individual must be based on the Word — and the Word alone.

(From a letter dated 4 June 1957 written on behalf of Shoghi Effendi to the National Spiritual Assembly of Canada)

162.   The believers must be encouraged to teach individually in their own homes. Bahá'u'lláh has enjoined upon the Bahá'ís the sacred obligation of teaching. We have no priests, therefore the service once rendered by priests to their religions is the service every single Bahá'í is expected to render individually to his religion. He must be the one who enlightens new souls, confirms them, heals the wounded and the weary upon the road of life, and gives them to quaff from the chalice of everlasting life the knowledge of the Manifestation of God in His Day.

(From a letter dated 5 July 1957 written on behalf of Shoghi Effendi to the National Spiritual Assembly of the Benelux countries)

163.   The Beloved Guardian directs me to inform you that you should not weary in well doing. He knows you must become discouraged at times when hardness of the hearts of the local people does not permit the budding of the seeds which you are so diligently sowing. However, he assures you that all of the seeds that are sown will ultimately reap their fruit...

(From a letter dated 7 August 1957 written on behalf of Shoghi Effendi to an individual believer)

164.   Teaching is the source of Divine Confirmation. It is not sufficient to pray diligently for guidance, but this prayer must be followed by meditation as to the best methods of action and *then action itself.* Even if the action should not immediately produce results, or perhaps not be entirely correct, that does not make so much difference, because *prayers can only be answered through action and if someone's action* is wrong, God can use that method of showing the pathway which is right....

(From a letter dated 22 August 1957 written on behalf of Shoghi Effendi to an individual believer)

165.   It is not enough for the friends to make the excuse that their best teachers and their exemplary believers have arisen and answered the call to pioneer. A "best teacher" and an "exemplary believer" is ultimately neither more nor less than an ordinary Bahá'í who has consecrated himself to the work of the Faith, deepened his knowledge and understanding of its Teachings, placed his

confidence in Bahá'u'lláh, and arisen to serve Him to the best of his ability. This door is one which we are assured will open before the face of every follower of the Faith who knocks hard enough, so to speak. When the will and the desire are strong enough, the means will be found and the way opened either to do more work locally, to go to a new goal town ... or to enter the foreign pioneer field....

The Bahá'ís are the leaven of God, which must leaven the lump of their nation. In direct ratio to their success will be the protection vouchsafed, not only to them but to their country. These are the immutable laws of God, from which there is no escape: "For unto whomsoever much is given, of him shall be much required."

(From a letter dated 21 September 1957 written on behalf of Shoghi Effendi to the National Spiritual Assembly of the United States)

TEACHING THE MASSES

A Compilation Prepared by the Research Department of the Universal
House of Justice
March 1968

TEACHING THE MASSES

Extracts from Letters of the Universal House of Justice and the Guardian

166. When the masses of mankind are awakened and enter the Faith of God, a new process is set in motion and the growth of a new civilization begins. Witness the emergence of Christianity and of Islám. These masses are the rank and file, steeped in traditions of their own, but receptive to the new Word of God, by which, when they truly respond to it, they become so influenced as to transform those who come in contact with them.

God's standards are different from those of men. According to men's standards, the acceptance of any cause by people of distinction, of recognized fame and status, determines the value and greatness of that cause. But, in the words of Bahá'u'lláh: "The summons and the message which We gave were never intended to reach or to benefit one land or one people only. Mankind in its entirety must firmly adhere to whatsoever hath been revealed and vouchsafed unto it." Or again, "He hath endowed every soul with the capacity to recognize the signs of God. How could He, otherwise, have fulfilled His testimony unto men, if ye be of them that ponder His Cause in their hearts." In countries where teaching the masses has succeeded, the Bahá'ís have poured out their time and effort in village areas to the same extent as they had formerly done in cities and towns. The results indicate how unwise it is to solely concentrate on one section of the population. Each National Assembly therefore should so balance its resources and harmonize its efforts that the Faith of God is taught not only to those who are readily accessible but to all sections of society, however remote they may be.

The unsophisticated people of the world — and they form the large majority of its population — have the same right to know of the Cause of God as others. When the friends are teaching the Word of God they should be careful to give the Message in the same simplicity as it is enunciated in our Teachings. In their contacts they must show genuine and divine love. The heart of an unlettered soul is extremely sensitive; any trace of prejudice on the part of the pioneer or teacher is immediately sensed.

When teaching among the masses, the friends should be careful not to emphasize the charitable and humanitarian aspects of the Faith as a means to win recruits. Experience has shown that when facilities such as schools, dispensaries, hospitals, or even clothes and food are offered to the people being taught, many complications arise. The prime motive should always be the response of man to God's message, and the recognition of His Messenger. Those who declare themselves as Bahá'ís should become enchanted with the beauty of the Teachings; and touched by the love of Bahá'u'lláh. The declarants need not know all the proofs, history, laws, and principles of the Faith, but in the process of declaring themselves they must, in addition to catching the spark of faith, become basically informed about the Central Figures of the Faith, as well as the existence of laws they must follow and an administration they must obey.

After declaration, the new believers must not be left to their own devices. Through correspondence and dispatch of visitors, through conferences and training courses, these friends must be patiently strengthened and lovingly helped to develop into full Bahá'í maturity. The beloved Guardian referring to the duties of Bahá'í Assemblies in assisting the newly declared believer has written: "...the members of each and every Assembly should endeavour, by their patience, their love, their tact and wisdom, to nurse, subsequent to his admission, the newcomer into Bahá'í maturity, and win him over gradually to the unreserved acceptance of whatever has been ordained in the teachings."

(From a letter dated 13 July 1964 written by the Universal House of Justice to all National Spiritual Assemblies)

167. From reports and minutes we receive from various National Spiritual Assemblies, it is evident that your efforts to attract a greater number of receptive souls to the Cause of God, to open new areas for increased teaching activity and to consolidate the work so far accomplished are dependent upon more local travelling teachers and pioneers being assisted by the Fund to spend more of their time in Bahá'í teaching services under your direction.

There is a danger in this situation which must be avoided at all costs. Despite the pressing requirements of the Nine Year Plan, no Bahá'í teacher anywhere should consider himself as permanently employed by the Faith. We do not have in the Cause of God any paid career open to Bahá'í teachers.

The beloved Guardian elucidated this basic principle of Bahá'í administration through his repeated letters to National Assemblies from which we quote:

At present it would be quite impossible to spread the Cause if those who arise to serve it as teachers or pioneers were not given financial assistance. All must realize, however, that the monies they receive are only to enable them to fulfil their objectives, and that they cannot consider themselves permanently entitled to be supported by the Cause.

(From a letter dated 12 August 1944 to the National Spiritual Assembly of the Bahá'ís of India and Burma)

Likewise travelling teachers should be assisted financially to carry out the "projects" assigned to them. The friends should not for a moment confuse this type of support with the creation of a paid clergy. Any Bahá'í can, at the discretion of the NSA receive this necessary assistance and it is clearly understood it is temporary and only to carry out a specific plan.

(From a letter dated 29 May 1946 to the National Spiritual Assembly of the British Isles)

Each National Assembly, through its auxiliary Teaching Committees, should be able to so plan the time and efforts of its band of subsidized travelling teachers that no impression of permanency is given. As far as possible each "project" must be definite in objective and in duration.

Likewise, when pioneer projects are envisaged, it must be made clear to the pioneer that he must make every effort to establish himself in some position in his pioneering post and thus become freed from the necessity of drawing further on Bahá'í funds.

Experience has shown that the observance of these principles is essential for the rearing of healthy communities; wherever they have been ignored difficulties and complications have arisen. In the application of these principles, if you have any difficulty, you should feel free to consult with us. Also, if you have found any particular scheme proving to be successful without violating the above principles, you are welcome to send the details to us so that we may share your methods with other National Assemblies and enable them to benefit from your experience.

Another problem closely linked with the above and which directly affects areas where mass teaching work is being carried out is the extent to which the local believers contribute to the Fund. As you note, one of the objectives of the Nine Year Plan is universal participation in Bahá'í community life. This can be possible when each believer understands that his personal spiritual life will be enriched and universal blessings will descend only if each Bahá'í participates in contributing, however poor he may be, however small the contribution, and in whatever form it is offered. Your Assembly must devote enough time at each meeting to consider carefully this basic process. We must be confident that the principles laid down in our Writings are not only workable, but are the only solution to the ills of mankind. With such confidence in their hearts, the members of each National Assembly faced with this stupendous problem must deliberate, and within the framework of the social and economic conditions of the communities they are serving, they must find ways and means that would gradually, yet positively, help in realising this purpose.

(From a letter dated 25 June 1964 written by the Universal House of Justice to all National Spiritual Assemblies engaged in teaching work among the masses)

168.　　It has been due to the splendid victories in large-scale conversion that the Faith of Bahá'u'lláh has entered a new phase in its development and establishment throughout the world. It is imperative, therefore, that the process of teaching the masses be not only maintained but accelerated. The teaching committee structure that each National Assembly may adopt to ensure best results in the extension of its teaching work is a matter left entirely to its discretion, but an efficient teaching structure there must be, so that the tasks are carried out with dispatch and in accordance with the administrative principles of our Faith. From among the believers native to each country, competent travelling teachers must be selected and teaching projects worked out. In the words of our beloved Guardian, commenting upon the teaching work in Latin America: "Strong and sustained support should be given to the vitally needed and highly meritorious activities started by the native ... travelling teachers, ... who, as the mighty task progresses, must increasingly bear the brunt of responsibility for the propagation of the Faith in their homelands."

While this vital teaching work is progressing each National Assembly must ever bear in mind that expansion and consolidation are inseparable processes that must go hand in hand. The inter-dependence of these processes is best elucidated in the following passage from the writings of the beloved

Guardian: "Every outward thrust into new fields, every multiplication of Bahá'í institutions, must be paralleled by a deeper thrust of the roots which sustain the spiritual life of the community and ensure its sound development. From this vital, this ever-present need attention must, at no time, be diverted; nor must it be, under any circumstances neglected, or subordinated to the no less vital and urgent task of ensuring the outer expansion of Bahá'í administrative institutions. That this community ... may maintain a proper balance between these two essential aspects of its development ... is the ardent hope of my heart...". To ensure that the spiritual life of the individual believer is continuously enriched, that local communities are becoming increasingly conscious of their collective duties, and that the institutions of an evolving administration are operating efficiently, is, therefore, as important as expanding into new fields and bringing in the multitudes under the shadow of the Cause.

These objectives can only be attained when each National Spiritual Assembly makes proper arrangements for all the friends to be deepened in the knowledge of the Faith. The National Spiritual Assemblies in consultation with the Hands of the Cause, who are the Standard-Bearers of the Nine Year Plan, should avail themselves of the assistance of Auxiliary Board members, who, together with the travelling teachers selected by the Assembly or its Teaching Committees, should be continuously encouraged to conduct deepening courses at Teaching Institutes and to make regular visits to Local Spiritual Assemblies. The visitors, whether Board members or travelling teachers should meet on such occasions not only with the Local Assembly but, of course, with the local community members, collectively at general meetings and even, if necessary, individually in their homes.

The subjects to be discussed at such meetings with the Local Assembly and the friends should include among others the following points:

1). the extent of the spread and stature of the Faith today;

2). the importance of the daily obligatory prayers (at least the short prayer);

3). the need to educate Bahá'í children in the Teachings of the Faith and encourage them to memorize some of the prayers;

4). the stimulation of youth to participate in community life by giving talks, etc. and having their own activities, if possible;

5). the necessity to abide by the laws of marriage, namely, the need to have a Bahá'í ceremony, to obtain the consent of parents, to observe monogamy; faithfulness after marriage; likewise the importance of abstinence from all intoxicating drinks and drugs;

6). the local Fund and the need for the friends to understand that the voluntary act of contributing to the Fund is both a privilege and a spiritual obligation. There should also be discussion of various methods that could be followed by the friends to facilitate their contributions and the ways open to the Local Assembly to utilize its local Fund to serve the interests of its community and the Cause;

7). the importance of the Nineteen Day Feast and the fact that it should be a joyful occasion and rallying point of the entire community;

8). the manner of election with as many workshops as required, including teaching of simple methods of balloting for illiterates, such as having one central home as the place for balloting and arranging for one literate person, if only a child, to be present at that home during the whole day, if necessary;

9). last but not least, the all-important teaching work, both in the locality and its neighbouring centres, as well as the need to continuously deepen the friends in the essentials of the Faith. The friends should be made to realize that in teaching the Faith to others they should not only aim at assisting the seeking soul to join the Faith, but also at making him a teacher of the Faith and its active supporter.

All the above points should, of course, be stressed within the framework of the importance of the Local Spiritual Assembly, which should be encouraged to vigorously direct its attention to these vital functions and become the very heart of the community life of its own locality, even if its meetings should become burdened with the problems of the community. The local friends should understand the importance of the law of consultation and realize that it is to the Local Spiritual Assembly that they should turn, abide by its decisions, support its projects, co-operate whole-heartedly with it in its task to promote the interests of the Cause, and seek its advice and guidance in the solution of personal problems and the adjudication of disputes, should any arise amongst the members of the community.

(From a letter dated 2 February 1966 written by the Universal House of Justice to all National Spiritual Assemblies engaged in mass teaching work)

169.   As it has already been pointed out, in various communications to you, it is important for the National Spiritual Assemblies to work out ways and means of creating a sense of belonging in the hearts of the believers. One of the ways this can be done is to bring to their attention the needs of the Fund.

The National Assembly should neither feel embarrassed nor ashamed in turning to the friends, continuously appealing to them to exemplify their faith and devotion to the Cause by sacrificing for it, and pointing out to them that they will grow spiritually through their acts of self-abnegation, that the fear of poverty should not deter them from sacrificing for the Fund, and that the assistance and bounty of the Source of all good and of all wealth are unfailing and assured.... It might be useful to share with the friends extracts from the writings of the beloved Guardian, such as the two passages we quote below:

Every Bahá'í, no matter how poor, must realize what a grave responsibility he has to shoulder in this connection, and should have confidence that his spiritual progress as a believer in the World Order of Bahá'u'lláh will largely depend upon the measure in which he proves, in deeds, his readiness to support materially the divine institutions of His Faith.

(From a letter dated 17 July 1937 written on behalf of the Guardian to the National Spiritual Assembly of the Bahá'ís of India and Burma)

The institution of the National Fund, so vital and essential for the uninterrupted progress of these activities must, in particular, be assured of the whole-hearted, the ever-increasing and universal support of the mass of believers, for whose welfare, and in whose name, these beneficent activities have been initiated and have been conducted. All, no matter how modest their resources, must participate.

(From a letter dated 8 August 1957 written on behalf of the Guardian to the National Spiritual Assembly of the Bahá'ís of Central and East Africa)

We feel that each National Assembly should carefully and regularly consult on this vital aspect of the education of the friends, spare no effort and lose no opportunity in bringing to their attention the needs of the hour. For example, where land is difficult to obtain, or where funds for the purchase of endowments are not available, the friends should be appealed to in a dignified and effective manner to donate from their own land for the use of Bahá'í institutions. In the construction of local Bahá'í centres, the National Assembly should carefully devise methods of appealing to the friends to contribute manpower or local materials for the construction of such buildings. If ready cash is not available for contributions to the Fund, the National Assembly should guide the friends in ways they could raise funds by a collective effort to cultivate a piece of land, by contributing cash crops, livestock or home-made dishes, sweetmeats, or handicrafts. Special meetings could also be arranged for the sale of such contributions in kind. In the matter of attendance of delegates at Conventions, the desirability of the friends themselves being self-supporting should be pointed out by the National Assembly. If a delegate cannot meet his own expenses in attending the Convention, the Local Assembly or the believers in the electoral unit from which the delegate comes should be encouraged by the National Assembly to defray such expenses, so that only when funds are unavailable from those sources, the National Assembly is approached to consider offering financial assistance. The same principle holds true about other activities, such as attendance at Institutes, Conferences and Summer Schools.

(From a letter dated 9 February 1967 written by the Universal House of Justice to various National Spiritual Assemblies)

170.   Many National Spiritual Assemblies in carrying out their plans for expansion and consolidation have found it necessary to select a number of believers for service as travelling teachers. While we appreciate the valuable services these travelling teachers have already rendered we are nevertheless deeply conscious of the problems facing your National Assemblies in your desire to carry out your teaching programmes with as much dispatch as possible. The purpose of this letter is to draw your attention to the fact that

these problems could well be minimized if the selection of such teachers were done with great care and discretion.

It must be realized that people who are mostly illiterate cannot have the benefit of reading for themselves the written word and of deriving directly from it the spiritual sustenance they need for the enrichment of their Bahá'í lives. They become dependent, therefore, to a large extent on their contacts with visiting teachers. The spiritual calibre or moral quality of these teachers assumes, therefore, great importance. The National Spiritual Assembly or the Teaching Committees responsible for the selection of these teachers should bear in mind that their choice must depend, not only on the knowledge or grasp of the teachings on the part of the teachers, but primarily upon their pure spirit and their true love for the Cause, and their capacity to convey that spirit and love to others.

...What wonderful results will soon be witnessed in the areas under your jurisdiction if you devise ways and means to ensure, as far as circumstances permit, that the travelling teachers you are encouraging to circulate among the friends will all be of the standard called for in these quotations — pure and sanctified souls, with nothing but true devotion and self-sacrifice motivating them in their services to God's Holy Cause....

(From a letter dated 26 October 1967 written by the Universal House of Justice to National Spiritual Assemblies engaged in mass teaching)

171. The paramount goal of the teaching work at the present time is to carry the message of Bahá'u'lláh to every stratum of human society and every walk of life. An eager response to the teachings will often be found in the most unexpected quarters, and any such response should be quickly followed up, for success in a fertile area awakens a response in those who were at first uninterested.

The same presentation of the teachings will not appeal to everybody; the method of expression and the approach must be varied in accordance with the outlook and interests of the hearer. An approach which is designed to appeal to everybody will usually result in attracting the middle section, leaving both extremes untouched. No effort must be spared to ensure that the healing Word of God reaches the rich and the poor, the learned and the illiterate, the old and the young, the devout and the atheist, the dweller in the remote hills and islands, the inhabitant of the teeming cities, the suburban businessman, the labourer in the slums, the nomadic tribesman, the farmer, the university student; all must be brought consciously within the teaching plans of the Bahá'í Community.

Whereas plans must be carefully made, and every useful means adopted in the furtherance of this work, your Assemblies must never let such plans eclipse the shining truth expounded in the enclosed quotations: that it is the purity of heart, detachment, uprightness, devotion and love of the teacher that attracts the divine confirmations and enables him, however ignorant he be in this world's learning, to win the hearts of his fellowmen to the Cause of God.

(From a letter dated 31 October 1967 written by the Universal House of Justice to all National Spiritual Assemblies)

172.   The growth of the Cause in India during the past several years has been vast and awe-inspiring, and it is quite natural that this growth should have been accompanied by problems and responsibilities that taxed the administrative experience and capacities of your National Assembly to the utmost.

...Travelling teachers and foreign pioneers could doubtless stimulate the friends and assist them in the teaching work, but essentially, the progress and growth of the Cause in India depend upon the services of your own people, and, to this end, a concerted effort should be made to integrate the friends in India into the work of the Cause in all its aspects, to assure universal participation that will result in winning even greater victories for the Cause. In this connection, your idea of engaging a number of well trained travelling teachers in India is, in principle, correct. You have various Teaching Institutes and a number of devoted, well-informed teachers at your disposal for this service. One of the most important duties of such travelling teachers should be to develop nuclei of devoted and active believers in the many centres who would inspire and assist the friends in active participation in the work to be done in their villages and towns. A plan should be developed to enable such travelling teachers to spend more time in fewer places instead of making brief visits in numerous centres. This would enable them to, in turn, train resident teachers in the various localities to spearhead the work of expansion and consolidation in their areas. The names of the believers thus trained should be given to the administrative bodies in charge of teaching. Teaching Institutes, Summer Schools, Conferences, etc. should be utilized to provide further encouragement and training for those believers whenever such opportunities arise.

In all your training programmes, the Bahá'í Administration should have special attention. The believers should know that our administration is part of our religion. For this reason, not only should you patiently and lovingly train the believers, but should also strive to attract to the Faith individuals who possess qualities and capacities that will add to the administrative strength of the Community as a whole. The beloved Guardian has stated: "There is no doubt that the poorer classes should be taught the Cause and given every opportunity to embrace it. More especially in order to demonstrate to people our cardinal lack of prejudice... However, he feels that the great point is to confirm people of true capacity and ability — from whatever social stratum they may be — because the Cause needs now, and will ever-increasingly need, souls of great ability who can bring it before the public at large, administer its ever-growing affairs, and contribute to its advancement in every field."

We note with deep satisfaction that the Message of God is being given to a cross-section of all the people of India, as evidenced by your success in attracting a large number of college students to the Faith, as well as others representing various classes of people.

(From a letter dated 15 February 1968 written by the Universal House of Justice to the National Spiritual Assembly of the Bahá'ís of India)

TEACHING PROMINENT PEOPLE

A Compilation Prepared by the Research Department of the Universal
House of Justice
September 1990

"It is the ardent prayer of the House of Justice that careful study of the passages included will assist the believers to appreciate the importance of fostering cordial relations with accomplished and distinguished figures, with people of capacity and with those occupying prominent positions in society. The aim of the believers should be to make of them friends of the Faith, dispelling any misconceptions they may have and unfolding before their eyes the vision of world solidarity and peace enshrined in the teachings of Bahá'u'lláh. The friends should be confident that the spiritually minded and receptive souls among such people will eventually accept the truth of the Bahá'í Revelation and join the ranks of its active supporters."

TEACHING PROMINENT PEOPLE

1. The Importance of Guiding "Distinguished Souls to The Cause"

From the Writings of 'Abdu'l-Bahá

173. I hope that thou wilt ... endeavour to teach some high-ranking and influential persons, for the hearts of the people have become attracted to the Cause of God and their minds bewildered and enthralled by its awesome grandeur. Those who occupy high positions, too, have become profoundly receptive to its message. The loved ones of God should therefore make a determined effort and guide these distinguished souls to the Cause.
(From a Tablet to an individual believer - translated from the Persian)

174. You should always seek to guide prominent people inasmuch as once such a person is regenerated he is likely to bring about the quickening of a thousand souls. Thus the spirit of truth would flow forth unimpeded into the veins and arteries of a multitude.
(From a Tablet to an individual believer - translated from the Persian)

175. Wherefore thou shouldst seek to impart the Message of influential persons and become a cause of guidance to the learned and distinguished, that perchance there may be raised up in Iran wise, sagacious souls who shall be solicitous for both the good of the state and the welfare of the populace, who shall labour diligently night and day to the end that their great nation may retrieve its former glory and restore for all the world to see the splendour of the Kíyáníyán kings, and that its illustrious people may shine out amongst mankind with an extraordinary brilliance and attain to lasting happiness and contentment.
(From a Tablet to a group of believers - translated from the Persian)

176. You should give serious concern to the matter of teaching, and think of ways of imparting the Message to prominent people, for once such persons have given their allegiance to the Faith they will cause the people to be led, troop after troop, to the wellspring of unfailing guidance.
(From a Tablet to an individual believer - translated from the Persian)

From letters written by or on behalf of Shoghi Effendi

177. It is incumbent upon the Bahá'ís to seize the opportunities of the present hour and, with wisdom, firm resolve and cheerfulness, impress the verities of their Faith upon the attention of every reasonable-minded person in whom they find a willingness to listen, explaining to them its noble principles, its universal teachings, its basic tenets, and the fundamental laws of the new era inaugurated by Bahá'u'lláh. In like manner, they must clearly and convincingly demonstrate to their fellow-citizens, whether high or low, the necessity of accepting and recognizing the resplendent teachings of the Universal Manifestation of God; must show to the leaders of their country that the unity, the strength and spiritual vitality of the Bahá'í community are palpable and concrete realities; must eliminate and nullify the effects of prejudices, superstitions, misunderstandings and all fanciful and erroneous conceptions on the hearts of the pure and righteous people; and must attract to the community of the Greatest Name, through whatever channels and by whatever means, persons of capacity, experience and devotion who, joining the ranks of the believers, severing themselves from every extraneous attachment, identifying themselves whole-heartedly with the organized community of the Bahá'ís in that area, will labour heart and soul to consolidate the foundations of Bahá'í belief and proclaim the tidings of the Promised Day. With regard to the Bahá'í literacy classes, their continuation at the present time is a service beyond measure both profitable and desirable. Similarly, the establishment of contact and maintenance of friendly relations with government officials and other nationally distinguished figures is a matter that should be regarded by the friends as a binding obligation.

(2 November 1928 written by Shoghi Effendi to the Iran Central Spiritual Assembly - translated from the Persian)

178. Shoghi Effendi was delighted to hear of your conversation with Sir ... How much he hopes to have such scholars obtain a true understanding of the spirit and teaching of the Cause and arise to dissipate that veil of misconceptions that is prejudicing the mind of the scholars in the western world. The Cause is in great need for such competent and spiritually minded men who after a thorough study of the Movement would share with the world the fruit of their labours.

(11 March 1929 written on behalf of Shoghi Effendi)

179.   ... he feels that the great point is to confirm people of true capacity and ability - from whatever social stratum they may be - because the Cause needs now, and will ever-increasingly need, souls of great ability who can bring it before the public at large, administer its ever-growing affairs, and contribute to its advancement in every field.

(30 October 1941 written on behalf of Shoghi Effendi)

180.   The more people of capacity who accept the Faith, the higher will become the standard of the entire group.

(17 June 1942 written on behalf of Shoghi Effendi)

181.   The Cause of God has room for all. It would, indeed, not be the Cause of God if it did not take in and welcome everyone - poor and rich, educated and ignorant, the unknown, and the prominent - God surely wants them all, as He created them all.

(10 December 1942 written on behalf of Shoghi Effendi)

182.   He was very pleased to learn ... that your reception was such a success, and that you now feel that people in high places are beginning to waken from their sleep and see the Light of Bahá'u'lláh. The time must come when they do; it just seems a question of how soon. A lot, also, depends on our having inside the Faith enough people of real capacity to form a nucleus that will attract to it similar souls ...

(22 November 1949 written on behalf of Shoghi Effendi)

183.   He hopes that your contact with Chief ... will prove fruitful, and that his heart may open to the Message you have carried him. It would be a great asset to the Faith if a prominent Chief of some tribe should accept it and arise to serve it.

(31 May 1952 written on behalf of Shoghi Effendi)

From letters written by the Universal House of Justice

184.   ... one of the most important duties of each National Spiritual Assembly is to acquaint leaders of thought and prominent men and women in its country with the fundamental aims, the history and the present status and achievements of the Cause. Such an activity must be carried out with the utmost wisdom, discretion and dignity.

(2 July 1967 to all National Spiritual Assemblies, published in Wellspring of Guidance, page 117)

185.   The paramount goal of the teaching work at the present time is to carry the message of Bahá'u'lláh to every stratum of human society and every walk of life. An eager response to the teachings will often be found in the most unexpected quarters, and any such response should be quickly followed up, for success in a fertile area awakens a response in those who were at first uninterested. The same presentation of the teachings will not appeal to everybody; the method of expression and the approach must be varied in accordance with the outlook and interests of the hearer. An approach which is designed to appeal to everybody will usually result in attracting the middle section, leaving both extremes untouched. No effort must be spared to ensure that the healing Word of God reaches the rich and the poor, the learned and the illiterate, the old and the young, the devout and the atheist, the dweller in the remote hills and islands, the inhabitant of the teeming cities, the suburban businessman, the labourer in the slums, the nomadic tribesman, the farmer, the university student; all must be brought consciously within the teaching plans of the Bahá'í Community.

(31 October 1967 to all National Spiritual Assemblies, published in Wellspring of Guidance, page 124)

186.   There have been notable advances in the process of gaining wider recognition for the Cause of God and in fostering cordial relations with civil authorities, a matter of vital importance in these days when there is a growth of opposition to the Faith from those who, misconstruing its true nature and aims, take alarm at its progress.

(Riḍván 1978 to the International Bahá'í Convention)

187.   Yet these disasters[1] have called forth fresh energies in the hearts of the friends, have fed the deep roots of the Cause and given rise to a great harvest

---

1   The "loss of six Hands of the Cause" and the "waves of bitter

of signal victories. Chief among these are the successful conclusion of the Five Year Plan; the launching of the Seven Year Plan, now in the final year of its second phase; and unprecedented proclamation of the Faith to Heads of States, parliaments and parliamentarians, government ministers and officials, leaders of thought and people prominent in the professions, resulting in a change of attitude on the part of the mass media, which now increasingly approach us for information about the Cause ...

The growing maturity of a world-wide religious community which all these processes indicate is further evidenced in the reaching out, by a number of national communities, to the social and economic life of their countries, exemplified by the founding of tutorial schools, the inception of radio stations, the pursuit of rural development programmes and the operation of medical and agricultural schemes. To these early beginnings must be added the undoubted skill acquired, as a result of the Iranian crisis, in dealing with international organizations, national governments and the mass media - the very elements of society with which it must increasingly collaborate toward the realization of peace on earth.

(Riḍván 1983 to the Bahá'ís of the World)

188. The entrance of the Cause onto the world scene is apparent from a number of public statements in which we have been characterized as "model citizens", "gentle", "law-abiding", "not guilty of any political offence or crime"; all excellent but utterly inadequate insofar as the reality of the Faith and its aims and purposes are concerned. Nevertheless people are willing to hear about the Faith, and the opportunity must be seized. Persistently greater and greater efforts must be made to acquaint the leaders of the world, in all departments of life, with the true nature of Bahá'u'lláh's revelation as the sole hope for the pacification and unification of the world. Simultaneous with such a programme must be unabated, vigorous pursuit of the teaching work, so that we may be seen to be a growing community, while universal observance by the friends of the Bahá'í laws of personal living will assert the fullness of, and arouse a desire to share in, the Bahá'í way of life. By all means the public

---

persecution" directed against the Bahá'í community in Iran.

image of the Faith will become, gradually but constantly, nearer to its true character ...

There can be no doubt that the progress of the Cause from this time onward will be characterized by an ever increasing relationship to the agencies, activities, institutions and leading individuals of the non-Bahá'í world. We shall acquire greater stature at the United Nations, become better known in the deliberations of governments, a familiar figure to the media, a subject of interest to academics, and inevitably the envy of failing establishments. Our preparation for and response to this situation must be a continual deepening of our faith, an unwavering adherence to its principles of abstention from partisan politics and freedom from prejudices, and above all an increasing understanding of its fundamental verities and relevance to the modern world.

(Riḍván 1984 to the Bahá'ís of the World)

2. Some Guidelines for Reaching Prominent People

2.1 "Establish Ties of Friendship"

From the Writings of 'Abdu'l-Bahá

189.   Some of the loved ones should establish ties of friendship with the notables of the region and manifest towards them the most affectionate regard. In this manner these men may become acquainted with the Bahá'í way of life, learn of the teachings of the Merciful One, and be informed of the pervasive influence of the Word of God in every quarter of the globe. If but one of these souls were attracted to the Cause, others would quickly be similarly moved, since the people tend to follow in the footsteps of their leaders.

(From a Tablet to an individual believer - translated from the Persian)

190.   Ye should strive to widen the circle of those with whom ye enjoy friendly relations, and to establish the closest contact with those benevolent souls whose only thought is to do good, who are labouring in the cause of universal peace, and who cherish no desire but to witness the unification of the world of humanity. Ye should seek out the company of such people as these, that ye may imbue them with an awareness of the heavenly Kingdom, for albeit their motives are of the finest, yet they do not realize that all the powers of the earth

are impotent either to establish universal peace or to promote the oneness of the human world. Nothing short of the power of the Word of God and the breaths of the Holy Spirit can ever succeed.

(From a Tablet to a Spiritual Assembly)

From letters written on behalf of Shoghi Effendi

191. Our Guardian hopes and prays that you will be guided in your endeavour to bring together at the banquet various prominent citizens of various races and religions with the sole purpose of winning them ultimately to the recognition of God's sacred Faith. You must stress the universal aspect of the Cause and show utmost kindness and love to them all as a preparation to their eventual acceptance of the entire truth.

(8 October 1927)

192. Some of the items were of great interest to him, especially that part which told of the contacts you have made with distinguished men and invited them to speak at your meetings. This is an effective way to make these take an active part in promoting the Faith and increasing their knowledge of its spirit and basic techniques.

Shoghi Effendi hopes that some day they will come forward as devoted servants and consecrate their lives to it ... there are distinguished men who are friends and admirers of the Cause, but due to their natural conservative and cautious attitude towards anything new, prefer to be onlookers than passionate advocates. They cannot however keep on that dispassionate state of mind, some day they will feel unwittingly drawn into it ... He is sending you two copies of *The Dawn-Breakers* to be presented to two distinguished friends of the Cause. One of these he wants to be presented to Sir ... in acknowledgment of the services he has rendered to us ... This is one form of keeping up the interest of such distinguished men in the progress of the Faith. Maybe one day they will take an active part.

(6 May 1932)

193. He was also very pleased to see that the Cause is receiving newspaper publicity there, and that you are winning the sympathetic interest of editors and people of importance. The Faith needs friends as well as adherents, and you should always endeavour to attract the hearts of enlightened leaders to its teachings.

(5 October 1945 to a Local Spiritual Assembly)

194.　There are, as you truly say, many important admirers of the Faith at present in the U.S.A. - and, indeed, in other countries, but it is unlikely such people will actually embrace the Cause; they are not ready to identify themselves with an as yet struggling Movement with a relatively small following; moreover, many such people would be unwilling to make the effort required to live up to Bahá'í standards of conduct! Still, it is excellent that we are winning more friends and admirers; this in itself helps the Cause and adds to its prestige, and gradually some of the people may actually make the sacrifice of entering its service.

(25 February 1947)

195.　He feels that the believers should make every effort, in the proper way and with discretion, to keep in contact with important people ... We should make every effort to ensure that leaders of thought in public life are not merely familiar with the name Bahá'í, but if possible stand in a cordial relationship to some members of our Community, if not to the body of the Faith.

(18 February 1951 to a National Spiritual Assembly)

From letters written by the Universal House of Justice

196.　A very important activity which has been pursued effectively in all too few countries is the undertaking by the National Spiritual Assembly of a sustained, planned effort to foster cordial relations with prominent people and responsible government officials and to familiarize them personally with the basic tenets and the teachings of the Faith. Such an activity must be carried out with wisdom and discretion, and requires the constant attention of a responsible committee as well as periodic review by the National Spiritual Assembly itself. Where successful it can effectively forestall opposition to the Faith and smooth the way for many essential aspects of the development of the Bahá'í community.

(Naw-Rúz 1974 to all National Spiritual Assemblies)

197. The House of Justice feels that your National Assembly must do more than distribute printed information about the Faith, as valuable as this is. A beginning should be made to identify the prominent persons in your country and ways be found to meet with them personally to acquaint them with the Faith. To this end, the House of Justice again urges you to appoint a committee to investigate the possibilities. If the few prominent Bahá'ís ... are too busy to assist, then you will have to either redirect their efforts or call others to this task.

(22 August 1984 to a National Spiritual Assembly)

2.2 Attitudes and Approaches

From the Writings of Bahá'u'lláh

198. Be righteous, O servants, in your actions! Turn not away from the helpless; make mention of me amidst the great, and have no fear.

(From a Tablet - translated from the Persian)

From the Writings of 'Abdu'l-Bahá

199. For we, the followers of the Blessed Beauty, should all be engaged in the service of the Cause of God, and become sources of guidance to humanity. Thou shouldst, if thou deemest it advisable and possible, proceed forthwith to organize a meeting of dignitaries. And when thy distinguished guests have assembled, speak to them about the Cause. Thou shouldst likewise advise the friends to arrange for another meeting with these same persons to be held one evening and to be addressed by them. This is a great service that I am entrusting to thee, and I pray to God that He may grant thee His assistance and confirmation, and bestow His blessings upon thy family.

(From a Tablet to an individual believer - translated from the Persian)

From letters written by or on behalf of Shoghi Effendi

200. I do hope your passionate fervour, your mature experience and the ardour of your love will accomplish a great deal among the higher-class people with whom you associate. The Cause must capture the heights, and I look to you as the beloved and enthusiastic apostle of 'Abdu'l-Bahá to win to the Cause, cultured and capable souls. Be not disheartened and be assured of my constant loving prayers for the success of your much-valued efforts.

(In the handwriting of Shoghi Effendi, appended to a letter dated 2 April 1925 written on his behalf)

201. Ever since its[2] inception Shoghi Effendi has cherished the hope of making it a work that would prove interesting and illuminating to the reader. Destined mainly for the non-Bahá'ís, he has tried to attract through its pages the attention of educated and enlightened people and especially leaders in every country, with a view to acquainting them with the broad and fundamental principles of the Faith and to winning their consideration of the Movement as a growing force for good and for peace throughout the entire world. It is therefore with lively satisfaction that he has seen the publication grow yearly in importance and this feeling has been lately enhanced very much by the words of interest and appreciation which he has received from many quarters and leading men, among which was a remarkably encouraging letter from Sir Herbert Samuel. Indeed Shoghi Effendi has made it a point to send copies to as many leading men as possible and copies of last year's issue were presented to the Emperor of Japan, the Sháh of Persia and Queen Marie of Rumania.

(12 December 1929 written on behalf of Shoghi Effendi)

202. As to teaching work in colleges and universities, this is very important, for students as a whole are open-minded and little influenced by tradition. They would easily enter the Cause if the subject is properly presented and their intellect and sentiments properly satisfied. This, however, should be attempted only by persons who have had university training and are therefore acquainted with the mind of the intelligent and educated youth.

(3 February 1932 written on behalf of Shoghi Effendi, published in Bahá'í News 64 (July 1932), page 4)

203. The letter you addressed to the Secretary of State, he liked very much. He sincerely hopes that through such approaches and communications the authorities will come to take into consideration the importance of the Cause and gradually feel deep sympathy and admiration for its spirit. It is very important that they should know how we stand and what is our attitude

---

2   The Bahá'í World

towards some of the outstanding problems and issues that face the world in the present day. These are very difficult questions and most delicate, but the Master's spirit will surely guide you and inspire you to do what is proper and wise.

(4 May 1932 written on behalf of Shoghi Effendi to the National Spiritual Assembly of the United States and Canada)

204. It is really strange how much modern thinkers are, of their own accord, drawing nearer to the teachings of the Faith and voicing views very much like ours. It shows clearly the truth of the saying of the Master that the spirit of the Movement has permeated the hearts of all the people of the world. It is God's hands operating and guiding the nations and intellectual men and leaders of society to a gradual acceptance of His Message revealed through Bahá'u'lláh.

The way we can hasten the development of this process is by doing our share in spreading the words of God far and wide. Even though we may not see any case of sudden conversion on the part of these intellectuals, yet they are bound to be influenced in their views and look to the Faith with greater admiration and with a more willing desire to be led by its precepts. Shoghi Effendi, therefore, wishes me to encourage you in your work, in sending appropriate literature to such men of learning.

(7 May 1933 written on behalf of Shoghi Effendi)

205. Through the reading of such a challenging and scholarly work[3] many will, undoubtedly, be awakened and stimulated, while others will be infuriated to the extent of virulently attacking the Faith. The unprecedented publicity which the Cause will be thus receiving will in itself constitute an important step towards a wider and fuller recognition of the Movement by distinguished personalities, in both intellectual and social circles.

(15 May 1934 written on behalf of Shoghi Effendi to a National Spiritual Assembly)

---

3   George Townshend, *The Promise of All Ages.*

206.   Regarding your work with the upper classes, the Guardian quite agrees with you that the people of wealth and culture do sometimes have a great capacity for spiritual things. But they need the right type of people to approach them, and a method that can suit their mentality. Our teaching methods should allow a certain degree of elasticity in establishing contacts with various types of individual seekers. Every inquirer has to be approached from his own angle. Those who are essentially of the mystic type should first be given those teachings of the Cause which emphasize the nature and value of spiritual realities; while those who are practically minded and of a positive type are naturally more ready and inclined to accept the social aspects of the Teachings. But of course, gradually the *entire* Message, in all its aspects and with the full implications it entails, should be explained to the newcomer. For to be a believer means to accept the Cause in its wholeness, and not to adhere to some of its teachings. However, as already stated, this ought to be done gradually and tactfully. For conversion is after all a slow process.

(28 December 1936 written on behalf of Shoghi Effendi)

207.   It is wonderful to see, at last, the intellectuals turning to the problems of the world and seeking to solve them. Side by side with this non-Bahá'í work, so close to many of Bahá'u'lláh's teachings, we believers must carry on our purely Bahá'í work, which only *we* can do, and which has such tremendous implications for the future of humanity in every sphere.

(14 April 1947 written on behalf of Shoghi Effendi)

208.   They[4] must be neither provocative nor supine, neither fanatical nor excessively liberal, in their exposition of the fundamental and distinguishing features of their Faith. They must be either wary or bold, they must act swiftly or mark time, they must use the direct or indirect method, they must be challenging or conciliatory, in strict accordance with the spiritual receptivity of the soul with whom they come in contact, whether he be a nobleman or a commoner, a northerner or a southerner, a layman or a priest, a capitalist or a socialist, a statesman or a prince, an artisan or a beggar. In their presentation of the Message of Bahá'u'lláh they must neither hesitate nor falter. They must

---

4   American pioneers.

be neither contemptuous of the poor nor timid before the great. In their exposition of its verities they must neither overstress nor whittle down the truth which they champion, whether their hearer belong to royalty, or be a prince of the Church, or a politician, or a tradesman, or a man of the street. To all alike, high or low, rich or poor, they must proffer, with open hands, with a radiant heart, with an eloquent tongue, with infinite patience, with uncompromising loyalty, with great wisdom, with unshakeable courage, the Cup of Salvation, at so critical an hour, to the confused, the hungry, the distraught and fear-stricken multitudes ...

(5 June 1947 written by Shoghi Effendi to the Bahá'ís of the West, published in Citadel of Faith, pages 25-6)

209.   The lack of prejudice, (for the most part) the true altruism of the pure scientist, is pretty well demonstrated, and to such people the Faith, if properly presented, should have a great appeal; and moreover such people could do tremendous things for the Cause if they joined it in numbers. There is certainly a place in the Cause for outstanding people, and we need more of them. But the administration must function on a consultative basis, not leadership.

(5 July 1947 written on behalf of Shoghi Effendi)

210.   It seems what we need now is a more profound and co-ordinated Bahá'í scholarship in order to attract such men as you are contacting. The world has - at least the thinking world - caught up by now with all the great and universal principles enunciated by Bahá'u'lláh over 70 years ago, and so of course it does not sound "new" to them. But we know that the deeper teachings, the capacity of His projected World Order to re-create society, are new and dynamic. It is these we must learn to present intelligently and enticingly to such men!

(3 July 1949 written on behalf of Shoghi Effendi)

211.   ... the solution given to the world's problems by Bahá'u'lláh is the only solution - being Divine in origin - and most desperately needed; therefore we, the few who have caught the vision, should not waste our energies beating up and down the paths pursued by humanity, and which are not solving its ghastly present-day problems. We should concentrate on the Cause, because it is what is needed to cure the world. This is a sound attitude, for if *we* don't devote ourselves to the Bahá'í work and teaching, who will? On the other hand there is a big difference between this and learning. If the Bahá'ís want to be really effective in teaching the Cause they need to be much better informed and able to discuss intelligently, intellectually, the present condition of the world and its problems. We need Bahá'í scholars, not only people far, far more deeply aware of what our teachings really are, but also well-read and well-educated people, capable of correlating our teachings to the current thoughts of the leaders of society.

We Bahá'ís should, in other words, arm our minds with knowledge in order to better demonstrate to, especially, the educated classes, the truths enshrined in our Faith. What the Guardian, however, does not advise the friends to do is to dissipate their time and energies in serving movements that are akin to our principles but not, we believe, capable of solving the present spiritual crisis the world finds itself in. We can co-operate with such movements and their promoters to good effect, while at the same time openly standing forth as Bahá'ís with a specific programme to offer society.

(5 July 1949 written on behalf of Shoghi Effendi)

From letters written by or on behalf of the Universal House of Justice

212.   In view of the difficulty you have experienced in obtaining publicity about the Faith in the national press in ..., the House of Justice has instructed us to say that there are three courses of action which should assist you in achieving this in the future. First, it is important that there be certain believers, such as the members of a public information committee, who are given the task of cultivating personal contacts with influential figures in the national information media. This personal contact is a vital element in fostering the receptivity of the media to news about the Faith. Secondly, as an aid to promoting such links, your representatives could take with them examples of excellent material about the Faith that has been published in such important newspapers as *Le Monde*, *The Times* of London, and *The New York Times* ... Thirdly, repeated mention of the Faith in the local press will contribute to the willingness of the national press to regard the Bahá'í Faith as newsworthy material.

(5 January 1981 written on behalf of the Universal House of Justice to a National Spiritual Assembly)

213.   With the approach of the Year of Peace and the rapidly growing awareness among thinking people of the need for world-wide solutions to the problems threatening humankind, the House of Justice feels that there is a need for research and the writing of books and papers on subjects which are of immediate interest to the leaders of thought and the generality of mankind.
(31 March 1985 written on behalf of the Universal House of Justice to the Association for Bahá'í Studies, Canada)

214.   It was also mentioned that there was a need to reach leaders of thought and people in authority with the Teachings; that there is a tendency for the people to more readily accept new ideas if they have already been accepted by the upper echelons of society. If this is so, perhaps a viable programme could be developed of inviting prominent Bahá'ís from other countries to visit ... in order to contact prominent [individuals] of similar station or profession.
(16 February 1987 written on behalf of the Universal House of Justice to a National Spiritual Assembly)

215.   National Bahá'í communities have organized and successfully conducted inter-religious conferences, peace seminars, symposiums on racism and other subjects on which we have a specific contribution to make, often achieving widespread publicity and the interest of highly placed leaders of society.
(Riḍván 1987 written by the Universal House of Justice to the Bahá'ís of the World)

2.3 The Role of the Spiritual Assemblies

From letters written by or on behalf of Shoghi Effendi

216.   To approach such well-known and important persons is always an extremely delicate matter, since it requires a good deal of wisdom, courage and ability. But those friends who really feel the urge to do so, and possess the necessary qualifications, should cultivate such friendships which, if properly done, can be of an immense benefit to the Cause. In any case, however, the assistance and help of either the Local or the National Assembly is not only useful but necessary, if important contacts of this sort are to be fruitful and promising ...
(30 August 1933 written on behalf of Shoghi Effendi)

217.   ... a resolute attempt should be made by the national elected representatives of the entire community, aided by their Public Relations, Race Unity, Public Meetings, Visual Education, College Speakers Bureau and Radio Committees, to reinforce the measures already adopted for the proclamation, through the press and radio, of the verities of the Faith to the masses, and for the establishment of closer contact with the leaders of public thought, with colleges and universities and with newspaper and magazine editors.

(5 June 1947 written by Shoghi Effendi to the Bahá'ís of the West, published in Citadel of Faith, pages 8-9)

218.   The National Assembly should not be timid about trying to contact important visitors to ... The stature of the Faith is now such that its representatives can demand and receive attention. Whether they are always successful or not, is not the point, the point is to let people of importance realize we are active and on the world scene, so to speak.

(23 November 1951 written on behalf of Shoghi Effendi to a National Spiritual Assembly)

219.   The Guardian was very happy to see your Assembly had had a successful meeting with both the Mayor of ... and the Minister for Foreign Affairs; such important contacts should be carried out on a high level, and only believers able to perhaps offer hospitality or having some point of contact with the officials in question or being themselves attractive to meet, should be used by your Assembly, and in conjunction with your members, to meet such personages.

(30 June 1952 written on behalf of Shoghi Effendi to a National Spiritual Assembly)

220.   He feels that the time has now come when you should establish a national committee to make contacts with civil authorities on a national level, and with important public figures in State and large City administrations. The purpose of these contacts is to establish friendly relations with important public figures, so that they may be fully informed of the Faith and its principles, may gain confidence in the Bahá'ís and their activities, may understand the non-political aspect of the Faith, and in the future, be anxious to be of assistance to us as the Faith evolves.

(29 December 1953 written on behalf of Shoghi Effendi to a National Spiritual Assembly)

From letters written by or on behalf of the Universal House of Justice

221.   National Spiritual Assemblies must promote wise and dignified approaches to people prominent in all areas of human endeavour, acquainting them with the nature of the Bahá'í community and the basic tenets of the Faith, and winning their esteem and friendship.

(Naw-Rúz 1979 written by the Universal House of Justice to the Bahá'ís of the World)

222.   ... the House of Justice is extremely happy that your National Assembly is continuing its wise, effective and ongoing efforts to familiarize the officials in your country about the Faith. Such approaches should be planned whenever the occasion arises. In the meantime, through your various proclamation efforts, the Bahá'í community should indirectly draw the attention of people of all strata of society to the Cause so that it will be easier for the Bahá'ís to have a positive access to the officials in the time of need.

(26 July 1987 written on behalf of the Universal House of Justice to a National Spiritual Assembly)

223.   The spark which ignited the mounting interest in the Cause of Bahá'u'lláh was the heroic fortitude and patience of the beloved friends in Iran, which moved the Bahá'í world community to conduct a persistent, carefully orchestrated programme of appeal to the conscience of the world. This vast undertaking, involving the entire community acting unitedly through its Administrative Order, was accompanied by equally vigorous and visible activities of that community in other spheres which have been detailed separately. Nonetheless, we are impelled to mention that an important outcome of this extensive exertion is our recognition of a new stage in the external affairs of the Cause, characterized by a marked maturation of National Spiritual Assemblies in their growing relations with governmental and non-governmental organizations and with the public in general. This recognition prompted a meeting in Germany last November of national Bahá'í external affairs representatives from Europe and North America, together

with senior representatives of the Offices of the Bahá'í International Community, intent on effecting greater co-ordination of their work. This was a preliminary step towards the gathering of more and more National Spiritual Assemblies into a harmoniously functioning, international network capable of executing global undertakings in this rapidly expanding field. Related to these developments was the significant achievement of international recognition accorded the Faith through its formal acceptance last October into membership of the Network on Conservation and Religion of the renowned World Wide Fund for Nature.

(Riḍván 1988 written by the Universal House of Justice to the Bahá'ís of the World)

2.4 The "Course of Prudence"

From the Writings of 'Abdu'l-Bahá

224. ... thou shouldst initially adopt that course of prudence that the Faith enjoins. In the early stages, thou shouldst seek out the company of the eminent members of the populace and, turning thyself in utter lowliness to the unseen realm of Glory, thou shouldst pray for succour and protection so that the Holy Spirit may, through the outpourings of its grace, grant thee its assistance. When, by thy godly conduct and demeanour, thy fervour, thy chaste and lucid utterance, thou shalt have succeeded in winning the affection of one and all, then shall the portals of heavenly guidance be opened wide; then shall the bounteous cup be borne around and all the souls that drink therefrom be inebriated with the wine of holy mysteries and truths.

(From a Tablet to an individual believer - translated from the Persian)

From letters written by or on behalf of Shoghi Effendi

225. You mentioned in your letter your intention to make contact with the representatives of movements which are akin to the Cause in the principles they advocate. Shoghi Effendi trusts that in all such communications and activities you would maintain the prestige and superiority of the Cause. We should never compromise our principles for some temporary benefits we are apt to reap. It is very important to bring the Cause to the attention of such leaders of thought and for this purpose we have to get in touch with them, but our aim should be to draw them to the Cause rather than follow their footsteps.

(26 November 1926 written on behalf of Shoghi Effendi to a National Spiritual Assembly)

226.   I entirely agree with you that non-interference in politics does not imply non-association on the part of the friends with the outside world. I hope you will impress the friends with the necessity of maintaining close, but not too intimate, relationships with the authorities, the foreign representatives, and the leaders of public thought in the capital. They should be on their guard, however, lest too close an association should lead, imperceptibly, to compromise on the principles which we cherish and uphold. They must mix with all classes of society without associating themselves with their policies and schemes.

(In the handwriting of Shoghi Effendi, appended to a letter dated 8 October 1927 written on his behalf)

227.   It is our supreme obligation to endeavour to bring the knowledge of this Revelation to the highest authorities and the leading personalities among our countrymen, but to refrain from associating ourselves or identifying our Faith with their political pursuits, their conflicting ambitions and party programmes. May the Almighty guide and sustain your high endeavours, and enable you to win for His Cause the most capable, the most virtuous and the most enlightened leaders of public opinion in that land.

(In the handwriting of Shoghi Effendi, appended to a letter dated 15 April 1932 written on his behalf)

228.   Shoghi Effendi fully approves your meeting of important men who are in power and have the reins of government in their hands. In fact he would urge you to avail yourself of every such opportunity that presents itself. But you should be very careful not to discuss matters that are political and that are points of contention between the different parties. That would drag the Cause into political affairs, a thing which was strictly forbidden by the Master. Your concern in meeting such people should be to familiarize them with the teachings of the Cause and imbue them with the spirit of the Movement. Should such men embrace the Movement they would lead with themselves thousands of others into the Cause.

(15 April 1932 written on behalf of Shoghi Effendi)

From a letter written by the Universal House of Justice

229. It is perfectly in order for Bahá'í institutions to present the Bahá'í view or recommendations on any subject of vital interest to the Faith which is under the consideration of a government, if the governmental authority itself invites such a submission, or if it is open to receive recommendations. The Bahá'í Assemblies should, however, refrain from bringing pressure to bear on the authorities in such matters, either separately or in concert with others. The Bahá'ís will submit their views, if permissible, expressing them as cogently and forcefully as the occasion warrants, but will not go beyond this to the stage of pressing the authorities to adopt these views. Moreover, when considering whether or not it is wise to make such a submission on any particular matter, the Bahá'í Assembly concerned must take care that it will not diffuse the energies of the Community or divert its resources by making submissions unless the interests of the Faith demand it. Likewise the Assembly must ensure that it does not, by any minute and detailed analysis of a situation, "needlessly alienate or estrange any government or people", or involve the Faith in "the base clamourings and contentions of warring sects, factions and nations".

(21 November 1971)

From letters written on behalf of the Universal House of Justice

230. The House of Justice received your letter of 13 December 1986 inquiring about permissible activities of the Bahá'ís in relation towards governments ... The general policy already enunciated by Shoghi Effendi in *The World Order of Bahá'u'lláh*, pages 63-67, should be scrupulously upheld by the friends. However, as the Faith emerges from obscurity, the application of certain aspects of this policy will require the clarification of the House of Justice. With the passage of time, practices in the political realm will definitely undergo the profound changes anticipated in the Bahá'í writings. As a consequence, what we understand now of the policy of non-involvement in politics will also undergo a change; but as Shoghi Effendi has written, this instruction, "at the present stage of the evolution of our Faith, should be increasingly emphasized, irrespective of its application to the East or to the West". In view of the necessity of the Bahá'í community to relate to governments, whether for reasons of defending its persecuted members or of responding to opportunities to be of service, a correct understanding of what is legitimate Bahá'í action in the face of the policy of non-interference with government affairs is bound to be difficult to achieve on the part of individual friends. The force of circumstances, operating internally and externally, is pressing the Bahá'í community into certain relationships with governments. Hence, it is important that decisions as to the conduct of such relationships be made by authorized institutions of the Faith and not by individuals. In matters of this kind, given the utter complexity of human affairs with which the Bahá'í community must increasingly cope both spiritually and practically, individual judgement is not sufficient.

(23 June 1987)

231.   This is a field of service in which much latitude for initiative must be given to individuals. For instance, in that aspect of the work which calls for reaching very important persons, it is necessary to rely on the personal relationships which individual Bahá'ís have developed or are capable of developing, to rely on their ability to engage the attention of such persons, because these Bahá'ís are themselves attractive in particular ways. While exercising careful judgement in selecting the individuals you can call on for such services, and providing them with any necessary guidance, you must also be sensitive to these points and avoid excessive control, or even the appearance of it, in your dealings with those who are engaged in these important services.

(26 April 1988 to a National Spiritual Assembly)

232.   Your comments concerning the maintenance of contacts with officials in the lower level of your Government's hierarchy are well taken, and you should feel confident in pursuing this wise course of action. There is no objection to initiating contact with high officials of the Catholic Church. This would require your careful consideration as to the timeliness of such action and determination by you as to how to proceed without unduly arousing opposition to the Faith. Your Assembly is encouraged to establish contacts with national associations, bearing in mind the need to select such organizations wisely, so as not to stretch your human and financial resources beyond reasonable bounds or to distract the community from its primary teaching efforts. As this balance is sometimes difficult to achieve, you may wish to include this as an element of your consultation with the Counsellors

on the role of ... in the process of the Faith's emergence from obscurity in Latin America and the world.

(23 March 1989 to a National Spiritual Assembly)

TEACHING INDIGENOUS PEOPLE

Extracts from the Writings of Shoghi Effendi or from Letters Written on His Behalf Regarding the Importance and Scope of the Teaching Work Among the Masses of Various Countries and their Aboriginal and Indigenous Inhabitants

Revised 1993

TEACHING INDIGENOUS PEOPLE

Extracts from the Writings of Shoghi Effendi or from Letters Written on His Behalf Regarding the Importance and Scope of the Teaching Work Among the Masses of Various Countries and their Aboriginal and Indigenous Inhabitants

233. Let any one who feels the urge among the participators in this crusade, which embraces all the races, all the republics, classes and denominations of the entire Western Hemisphere, arise, and, circumstances permitting, direct in particular the attention, and win eventually the unqualified adherence, of the Negro, the Indian, the Eskimo, and Jewish races to his Faith. No more laudable and meritorious service can be rendered the Cause of God, at the present hour, than a successful effort to enhance the diversity of the members of the American Bahá'í community by swelling the ranks of the Faith through the enrolment of the members of these races. A blending of these highly differentiated elements of the human race, harmoniously interwoven into the fabric of an all-embracing Bahá'í fraternity, and assimilated through the dynamic process of a divinely-appointed Administrative Order, and contributing each its share to the enrichment and glory of Bahá'í community life, is surely an achievement the contemplation of which must warm and thrill every Bahá'í heart...

(From a letter dated 25 December 1938 written by Shoghi Effendi to the Bahá'ís of the United States and Canada, published in "The Advent of Divine Justice" (Wilmette: Bahá'í Publishing Trust, 1984), p. 54)

234. Smallness of numbers, lack of skilled teachers, and modesty of means should not discourage or deter them. They must remember the glorious history of the Cause, which...was established by dedicated souls who, for the most part, were neither rich, famous, nor well educated, but whose devotion, zeal and self-sacrifice overcame every obstacle and won miraculous victories for the Faith of God. Such spiritual victories can now be won for India and Burma by the friends. Let them dedicate themselves - young and old, men and women alike - and go forth and settle in new districts, travel, and teach in spite of lack of experience, and be assured that Bahá'u'lláh has promised to aid all those

who arise in His Name. His strength will sustain them; their own weakness
is unimportant.

*(From a letter dated 29 June 1941 written on behalf of Shoghi Effendi to
the National Spiritual Assembly of India and Burma)*

235.   Many are the souls who, in this Holy Cause, without either worldly means
or knowledge, have set ablaze the hearts of others with the divine love and
rendered the Faith imperishable services. The Guardian hopes that you will
be able to do likewise.

*(From a letter dated 5 October 1941 written on behalf of Shoghi Effendi to
an individual believer)*

236.   There is no doubt that the poorer classes should be taught the Cause and
given every opportunity to embrace it. More especially in order to demonstrate
to people our cardinal lack of prejudice, class prejudice as much as any other
kind of prejudice. However he feels that the great point is to confirm people
of true capacity and ability - from whatever social stratum they may be -
because the Cause needs now, and will ever-increasingly need, souls of great
ability who can bring it before the public at large, administer its ever-growing
affairs, and contribute to its advancement in every field.

*(From a letter dated 30 October 1941 written on behalf of Shoghi Effendi
to an individual believer)*

237.   That is perhaps what is most glorious about our present activities all over
the world, that we, a band not large in numbers, not possessing financial
backing or the prestige of great names, should, in the name of our beloved
Faith, be forging ahead at such a pace, and demonstrating to future and present
generations that it is the God-given qualities of our religion that are raising it
up and not the transient support of worldly fame or power. All that will come
later, when it has been made clear beyond the shadow of a doubt that what
raised aloft the banner of Bahá'u'lláh was the love, sacrifice, and devotion of
His humble followers and the change that His teachings wrought in their
hearts and lives.

*(From a letter dated 20 June 1942 written on behalf of Shoghi Effendi to
the National Spiritual Assembly of the British Isles)*

238.   The initial contact already established, the concluding years of the first Bahá'í century, in obedience to 'Abdu'l-Bahá's Mandate, with the Cherokee and Oneida Indians in North Carolina and Wisconsin, with the Patagonian, the Mexican and the Inca Indians, and the Mayans in Argentina, Mexico, Peru and Yucatán, respectively, should, as the Latin American Bahá'í communities gain in stature and strength, be consolidated and extended. A special effort should be exerted to secure the unqualified adherence of members of some of these tribes to the Faith, their subsequent election to its councils, and their unreserved support of the organized attempts that will have to be made in the future by the projected National Assemblies for the large-scale conversion of Indian races to the Faith of Bahá'u'lláh.

...

Nor should any of the pioneers, at this early stage in the upbuilding of Bahá'í national communities, overlook the fundamental prerequisite for any successful teaching enterprise, which is to adapt the presentation of the fundamental principles of their Faith to the cultural and religious backgrounds, the ideologies, and the temperament of the divers races and nations whom they are called upon to enlighten and attract. The susceptibilities of these races and nations,...differing widely in their customs and standards of living, should at all times be carefully considered, and under no circumstances neglected.

(From a letter dated 5 June 1947 written by Shoghi Effendi to the Bahá'í's of the West)

239.   The primary reason for anyone to becoming a Bahá'í must of course be because he has come to believe the doctrines, the teachings and the Order of Bahá'u'lláh are the correct thing for this stage in the world's evolution. The Bahá'ís themselves as a body have one great advantage: they are sincerely convinced Bahá'u'lláh is right; they have a plan, and they are trying to follow it. But to pretend they are perfect, that the Bahá'ís of the future will not be a hundred times more mature, better balanced, more exemplary in their conduct, would be foolish.

(From a letter dated 5 July 1947 written on behalf of Shoghi Effendi to an individual believer)

240.   The news of the very successful Congress held in Santiago pleased him very much. Now that more of the Latin believers are active and beginning to assume responsibilities, the work will go forward on a more permanent foundation, as pioneers from a foreign land can never take the place of native believers who must always constitute the bedrock of any future development of the Faith in their country.

(From a letter dated 30 January 1948 written on behalf of Shoghi Effendi to an individual believer)

241.   ...great patience must be used in dealing with the childlike members of some of these primitive races. They are innocent in heart and have certainly had a very bad example, in many Christians, of a purely mercenary approach to religion; but if their hearts and minds once become illumined with the Faith they could make very fine believers.

(From a letter dated 29 April 1948 written on behalf of Shoghi Effendi to the National Spiritual Assembly of the British Isles)

242.   We can truly say that this Cause is a cause that enables people to achieve the impossible! For the Bahá'ís, everywhere, for the most part, are people with no great distinguishments of either wealth or fame, and yet once they make the effort and go forth in the name of Bahá'u'lláh to spread His Faith, they become, each one, as efficacious as a host! Witness what Mustafa Roumie accomplished in Burma, and a handful of pioneers achieved, in a decade, in Latin America! It is the quality of devotion and self-sacrifice that brings rewards in the service of this Faith rather than means, ability or financial backing.

(From a letter dated 11 May 1948 written on behalf of Shoghi Effendi to the National Spiritual Assembly of Australia and New Zealand)

243.   The work being done by various Bahá'ís, including our dear Indian believer who returned from the United States in order to pioneer amongst his own people, in teaching the Canadian Indians, is one of the most important fields of activity under your jurisdiction. The Guardian hopes that ere long many of these original Canadians will take an active part in Bahá'í affairs and arise to redeem their brethren from the obscurity and despondency into which they have fallen.

(From a letter dated 23 June 1950 written on behalf of Shoghi Effendi to the National Spiritual Assembly of Canada)

244.   Every outward thrust into new fields, every multiplication of Bahá'í institutions, must be paralleled by a deeper thrust of the roots which sustain the spiritual life of the community and ensure its sound development. From this vital, this ever-present need attention must, at no time, be diverted; nor must it be, under any circumstances, neglected, or subordinated to the no less vital and urgent task of ensuring the outer expansion of Bahá'í administrative institutions. That this community...may maintain a proper balance between these two essential aspects of its development...is the ardent hope of my heart...

(From a letter dated 30 December 1948 written on behalf of Shoghi Effendi to the National Spiritual Assembly of Australia and New Zealand)

245.   Shoghi Effendi is also most anxious for the Message to reach the aboriginal inhabitants of the Americas. These people, for the most part downtrodden and ignorant, should receive from the Bahá'ís a special measure of love, and every effort be made to teach them. Their enrolment in the Faith will enrich them and us, and demonstrate our principle of the Oneness of man far better than words or the wide conversion of the ruling races ever can.

(From a letter dated 11 July 1951 written on behalf of Shoghi Effendi to the National Spiritual Assembly of Meso-America and Antilles)

246.   Your Assembly is called upon to direct and safeguard the activities of our Faith in a truly vast and impressive area. But the very newness of the work, the room for spiritual conquest, the great need of the people, both aboriginal and European in origin, to hear of Bahá'u'lláh, is stimulated and challenging, and must call forth the best in every believer.

...

The Guardian feels that special efforts must be made to enrol the primitive peoples of South America in the Cause. These souls, often so exploited and despised, deserve to hear of the Faith, and will become a great asset to it once their hearts are enlightened.

(From a letter dated 11 July 1951 written on behalf of Shoghi Effendi to the National Spiritual Assembly of South America)

247.   He was very pleased to hear of initial steps you have taken to teach the Indians.

He adds one suggestion (he does not know if it is practicable or not): can contact not be made with Indians who have become more or less absorbed into the life of the white element of the country and live in or visit the big cities? These people, finding the Bahá'ís <u>sincerely</u> lacking in either prejudice .. or that even worse attitude, condescension .. might not only take interest in our Teachings, but also help us to reach their people in the proper way.

It is a great mistake to believe that because people are illiterate or live primitive lives, they are lacking in either intelligence or sensibility. On the contrary, they may well look on us, with the evils of our civilization, with its moral corruption, its ruinous wars, its hypocrisy and conceit, as people who merit watching with both suspicion and contempt. We should meet them as equals, well-wishers, people who admire and respect their ancient descent, and who feel that they will be interested, as we are, in a <u>living religion</u> and not in the dead forms of present-day churches.

(From a letter dated 21 September 1951 written on behalf of Shoghi Effendi to the Comite Nacional de Ensenanza Bahai para los Indigenas)

248.   The Guardian was most happy to hear of the excellent work some of the Bahá'ís are doing with the Eskimos and the Indians, and considers their spirit most exemplary. They are rendering a far greater service than they, themselves, are aware of, the fruits of which will be seen, not only in Canada, but because of their repercussions, in other countries where primitive populations must be taught.

(From a letter dated 8 June 1952 written on behalf of Shoghi Effendi to the National Spiritual Assembly of Canada)

249.   He was particularly pleased to see that members of your Assembly have been out travelling and contacting the friends in an effort to deepen their understanding of the workings of the administration and also their knowledge of the Faith in general. He feels that particularly at present in Latin America this intimate, loving and friendly approach will do more to further the work than anything else. Indeed, he would go so far as to advise your Assembly to avoid deluging the friends with circulars and unnecessary bulletins. You must always bear in mind the genuine difference between the peoples of the south and the peoples of the north; to use the same techniques as those adopted in the United States would be disastrous because the mentality and background of life are quite different.   Much as the friends need administration, it must be brought to them in a palatable form, otherwise they will not be able to assimilate it and instead of consolidating the work you will find some of the believers become estranged from it.

Whenever you feel at all discouraged you should remember how many years it took for the administration to get as well established as it is at present in North America. Problems repeat themselves and in the earlier stages in the U.S.A. the body of the believers was very loosely knit together, many of the friends were, as they now are in Latin America, affiliated with various more or less progressive cults from which they had come to the Faith from which they could not be suddenly cut off; they had to be weaned and educated; the same thing you must now do. He urges you therefore to be very patient with the believers, and, through loving consultation and education, gradually insist that the old allegiances must give way to the great and all-satisfying bond they have now found with Bahá'u'lláh and His Faith.

Mature teachers are the greatest need of the Faith everywhere, and no doubt in your area too. One wise and dedicated soul can so often give life to an inactive community, bring in new people and inspire to greater sacrifice. He hopes that whatever else you are able to do during the coming months, you will be able to keep in circulation a few really good Bahá'í teachers.

(From a letter dated 30 June 1952 written on behalf of Shoghi Effendi to the National Spiritual Assembly of South America)

250.   He fully appreciates the fact that the believers are still somewhat attached to the different cults from which they have come; this is a problem which always faces the Faith in a new region; it existed a long time in America, and seems part of the growth of the Cause. He feels your Assembly can afford to be patient with the friends, while at the same time educating them into a deeper understanding of the Cause. As their awareness of the true significance of Bahá'u'lláh grows, they will become weaned form the old ideas and give full allegiance to His teachings.

(From a letter dated 30 June 1952 written on behalf of Shoghi Effendi to the National Spiritual Assembly of South America)

251.   REJOICE SHARE BAHÁ'Í COMMUNITIES EAST WEST THRILLING REPORTS FEATS ACHIEVED HEROIC BAND BAHÁ'Í PIONEERS LABOURING DIVERS WIDELY SCATTERED AFRICAN TERRITORIES... REMINISCENT ALIKE EPISODES RELATED BOOK

ACTS RAPID DRAMATIC PROPAGATION FAITH INSTRUMENTALITY DAWN-BREAKERS HEROIC AGE BAHÁ'Í DISPENSATION. MARVELLOUS ACCOMPLISHMENTS SIGNALIZING RISE ESTABLISHMENT ADMINISTRATIVE ORDER FAITH LATIN AMERICA ECLIPSED. EXPLOITS IMMORTALIZING RECENTLY LAUNCHED CRUSADE EUROPEAN CONTINENT SURPASSED...NUMBER AFRICANS CONVERTED COURSE LAST FIFTEEN MONTHS...PROTESTANT CATHOLIC PAGAN BACKGROUNDS LETTERED UNLETTERED BOTH SEXES REPRESENTATIVE NO LESS SIXTEEN TRIBES PASSED TWO HUNDRED MARK. EFFULGENT RAYS GOD'S TRIUMPHANT CAUSE ... FAST AWAKENING CONTINENT PENETRATING ACCELERATING RATE ISOLATED REGIONS UNFREQUENTED WHITE MEN ENVELOPING THEIR RADIANCE SOULS HITHERTO INDIFFERENT PERSISTENT HUMANITARIAN ACTIVITIES CHRISTIAN MISSIONS CIVILIZING INFLUENCE CIVIL AUTHORITIES.

(From a cable dated 5 January 1953 by Shoghi Effendi to the National Spiritual Assembly of the United States)

252. I hail with joyous heart the convocation in the heart of the African continent of the first of the four Intercontinental Teaching Conferences constituting the highlights of the world-wide celebrations for the Holy Year which commemorates the hundredth anniversary of the birth of the Mission of the Founder of our Faith. I welcome with open arms the unexpectedly large number of representatives of the pure-hearted and the spiritually receptive Negro race, so dearly loved by 'Abdu'l-Bahá, for whose conversion to His Father's Faith He so deeply yearned and whose interests He so ardently championed in the course of His memorable visit to the North American continent. I am reminded, on this historic occasion, of the significant works uttered by Bahá'u'lláh Himself, Who, as attested by the Centre of the Covenant, in His Writings, "compared the coloured people to the black pupil of the eye", through which "the light of the spirit shineth forth". I feel particularly gratified by the substantial participation in this epoch-making Conference of the members of a race dwelling in a continent which for the most part has retained its primitive simplicity and remained uncontaminated by the evils of a gross, and rampant and cancerous materialism undermining the fabric of human society alike in the East and in the West, eating into the vitals of the conflicting peoples and races inhabiting the American, the European and the Asiatic continents, and alas threatening to engulf in one common catastrophic convulsion the generality of mankind. I acclaim the preponderance of the members of this same race at so significant a Conference, a phenomenon unprecedented in the annals of Bahá'í Conferences held during over a century, and auguring well for a corresponding multiplication in the number of the representatives of the yellow, the red and brown races of mankind dwelling respectively in the Far East, in the Far West and in the islands of the South Pacific Ocean, a multiplication designed ultimately to bring to a proper equipoise the divers ethnic elements comprised within the highly diversified world-embracing Bahá'í Fellowship.

(From a letter dated February 1953 to the African Intercontinental Teaching Conference)

253. He hopes that, during this coming year, you ... will devote yourselves as much as you can to consolidating the new Assemblies, and assisting the new believers to gradually understand better the Administration, and its application in Bahá'í Community life. Tact, love and patience will no doubt be needed, and one cannot expect these new believers to do everything in the same way that old and tried Communities do. Indeed, individuality of expression, within the framework of the Administrative Order, is preferable to great uniformity.

(From a letter dated 26 April 1953 written on behalf of Shoghi Effendi to an individual believer)

254. He was very happy to know that Charlottetown not only achieved Assembly status, but that the believers there are most self-supporting, as this is a sound basis for the expansion of the work in any place, especially in such a difficult one.

(From a letter dated 20 June 1953 written on behalf of Shoghi Effendi to the National Spiritual Assembly of Canada)

255. He feels that a great potential strength lies in these new African believers. No doubt your Committee will be faced with problems, due to the inexperience of some of these people in administrative matters, but, through loving guidance, and the wisdom of those who are associated with them on the spot, these minor things can be satisfactorily taken care of, and the main thing, the establishment of Assemblies and Groups, be carried out successfully.

(From a letter dated 4 June 1953 written on behalf of Shoghi Effendi to the National Spiritual Assembly of the British Isles Africa Committee)

256.   When enrolling new believers, we must be wise and gentle, and not place so many obstacles in their way that they feel it impossible to accept the Faith. On the other hand, once accorded membership in the Community of the followers of Bahá'u'lláh, it must be brought home to them that they are expected to live up to His teachings, and to show forth the signs of a noble character in conformity with His Laws. This can often be done gradually, after the new believer is enrolled.

(From a letter dated 25 June 1953 written on behalf of Shoghi Effendi to the National Spiritual Assembly of the British Isles)

257.   It must, as it gathers momentum, awaken the select and gather the spiritually hungry amongst the peoples of the world, as well as create an awareness of the Faith not only among the political leaders of present-day society but also among the thoughtful and the erudite in other spheres of human activity. It must, as it approaches its climax, carry the torch of the Faith to regions so remote, so backward, so inhospitable that neither the light of Christianity or Islám has, after the revolution of centuries, as yet penetrated. It must, as it approaches its conclusion, pave the way for the laying, on an unassailable foundation, of the structural basis of an Administrative Order whose fabric must, in the course of successive Crusades, be laboriously erected throughout the entire globe, and which must assemble beneath its sheltering shadow peoples of every race, tongue, creed, colour and nation.

...

...winning to the Faith fresh recruits to the slowly yet steadily advancing army of the Lord of Hosts...is so essential to the safeguarding of the victories which the band of heroic Bahá'í conquerors are winning in the course of their several campaigns in all the continents of the globe.

Such a steady flow of reinforcements is absolutely vital and is of extreme urgency, for nothing short of the vitalizing influx of new blood that will reanimate the world Bahá'í Community can safeguard the prizes which, at so great a sacrifice, involving the expenditure of so much time, effort and treasure, are now being won in virgin territories by Bahá'u'lláh's valiant Knights, whose privilege is to constitute the spearhead of the onrushing battalions which, in divers theatres and in circumstances often adverse and extremely challenging, are vying with each other for the spiritual conquest of the unsurrendered territories and islands on the surface of the globe.

This flow, moreover, will presage and hasten the advent of the day which, as prophesied by 'Abdu'l-Bahá, will witness the entry by troops of peoples of divers nations and races into the Bahá'í world - a day which, viewed in its proper perspective, will be the prelude to the long-awaited hour when a mass conversion on the part of these same nations and races, and as a direct result of a chain of events, momentous and possibly catastrophic in nature and which cannot as yet be even dimly visualized, will suddenly revolutionize the fortunes of the Faith, derange the equilibrium of the world, and reinforce a thousandfold the numerical strength as well as the material power and the spiritual authority of the Faith of Bahá'u'lláh.

(From a letter dated 25 June 1953 written on behalf of Shoghi Effendi to the National Spiritual Assembly of the United States)

258. The beloved Guardian was greatly delighted to learn of the success of the institute for teaching the Indian children. He feels this is a very fine method of implanting the teachings of the Faith in the hearts and minds of the young children, so that they may grow and develop into strong and virile men and women who will serve the Cause. Likewise through this effort, he hopes you will be able to attract some of the parents.

(From a letter dated 18 February 1954 written on behalf of Shoghi Effendi to an individual believer)

259. The spirit of the African believers is very touching, very noble, and indeed presents a challenge of their fellow-Bahá'ís all over the world. It seems that God has endowed these races, living in the so-called "dark" continent, with great spiritual faculties, and also with mental faculties, which, as they mature in the Faith, will contribute immensely to the whole, throughout the Bahá'í world.

...

In your communications to the Bahá'ís of Uganda please assure them of the Guardian's prayers, of his deep affection for them, and tell them that he is proud of them, of their spirit and of their achievements.

(From a letter dated 11 May 1954 written on behalf of Shoghi Effendi to the Uganda Teaching Committee)

260.   ...the whole object of the pioneers in going forth to Africa, is to teach the coloured people, and not the white people. This does not mean that they must refuse to teach the white people, which would be a foolish attitude. It does, however, mean that they should constantly bear in mind that it is to the native African that they are now carrying the Message of Bahá'u'lláh, in his own country, and not to people from abroad who have migrated there permanently or temporarily and are the minority, and many of them, judging by their acts, a very unsavoury minority.

...

Africa is truly awakening and finding herself, and she undoubtedly has a great message to give, and a great contribution to make to the advancement of world civilization. To the degree to which her peoples accept Bahá'u'lláh, will they be blessed, strengthened and protected.

(From a letter dated 4 June 1954 written on behalf of Shoghi Effendi to the National Spiritual Assembly of the British Isles Africa Committee)

261.   In connection with the teaching work throughout the Pacific area, he fully believes that in many cases the white society is difficult to interest in anything but its own superficial activities. The Bahá'ís must identify themselves on the one hand, as much as they reasonably can, with the life of the white people, so as not to become ostracized, criticized and eventually ousted from their hard-won pioneer posts. On the other hand, they must bear in mind that the primary object of their living there is to teach the native population the Faith. This they must do with tact and discretion, in order not to forfeit their foothold in these islands which are often so difficult of access.

Sound judgement, a great deal of patience and forbearance, faith and nobility of conduct, must distinguish the pioneers, and be their helpers in accomplishing the object of their journey to these far places.

(From a letter dated 16 June 1954 written on behalf of Shoghi Effendi to the National Spiritual Assembly of Australia and New Zealand)

262. In dealing with people who are still backward in relation to our civilized standards, and in many cases guided by a tribal system which has strong orders of its own, he feels that you should be both tactful and forbearing...we must not be too strict in enforcing our opinions on peoples still living in primitive social orders.

(From a letter dated 17 June 1954 written on behalf of Shoghi Effendi to the National Spiritual Assembly of the British Isles)

263. He feels teaching work in Uganda should now be concentrated on consolidation, primarily.

(From a letter dated 13 December 1955 written on behalf of Shoghi Effendi to the National Spiritual Assembly of the British Isles)

264. Above all, the utmost endeavour should be exerted by your Assembly to familiarize the newly enrolled believers with the fundamental and spiritual verities of the Faith, and with the origins, the aims and purposes, as well as the processes of a divinely appointed Administrative Order, to acquaint them more fully with the history of the Faith, to instil in them a deeper understanding of the Covenants of both Bahá'u'lláh and of 'Abdu'l-Bahá, to enrich their spiritual life, to rouse them to a greater effort and a closer participation in both the teaching of the Faith and the administration of its activities, and to inspire them to make necessary sacrifices for the furtherance of its vital interests. For as the body of the avowed supporters of the Faith is enlarged, and the basis of the structure of its Administrative Order is broadened, and the fame of the rising community spreads far and wide, a parallel progress must be achieved, if the fruits already garnered are to endure, in the spiritual quickening of its members and the deepening of their inner life.

(From a letter dated 26 June 1956 written on behalf of Shoghi Effendi to the National Spiritual Assembly of Canada)

265. Some of the territories are practically exclusively Arab with a European minority, with Muslim background and an advanced civilization and culture of their own. They must be approached with teaching methods suitable to the mentality of the people. On the other hand, many of the other countries represent a backward people, from the standpoint of modern civilization, but people much more receptive in heart and soul to the Teachings of Bahá'u'lláh, much more sensitive to spiritual values, much readier indeed to embrace the Message of Bahá'u'lláh and arise in its service, as we have seen so wonderfully demonstrated during the last four years in the history of the Cause in Africa. These people must also be taught in a way that will attract them to the Cause.

The African Bahá'ís already enrolled will require deepening in the Administration during the coming years, in order to better fit them for the day which must inevitably come when each protectorate, country and island will possess its own National Spiritual Assembly. To the degree to which your Assembly succeeds in laying a firm foundation at the present time, will depend the rapidity of the unfoldment of the Faith in these different countries and the readiness of the believers to shoulder independently their national Bahá'í work.

As he has mentioned many times to pilgrims and in his communications to friends in North Africa, he wishes special attention paid in the area to the Berbers. Indeed every effort should be made to enrol as many Berber minorities in the Faith as possible, as well as the other races among the inhabitants of the country.

(From a letter dated 2 July 1956 written on behalf of Shoghi Effendi to the National Spiritual Assembly of North West Africa)

266.　　The most important work of all is to train the African believers as teachers and administrators, so that they can carry the Message to their own people, and be in a position to lay firm and enduring foundations for the future Assemblies throughout all these vast territories. Every other activity falls into insignificance compared to this one.

It is only natural that the help and advice of the pioneers should be required for some time to come, owing to their long experience in the Faith and their deeper knowledge of its Teachings, due to, not only the length of time they have been Bahá'ís and able to study them, but to the fact that so many of the Teachings are in English and they could study them.

The translation of ever more literature into African tongues is likewise very important, as the new believers are ready and eager to learn, and must have the facilities placed at their disposal.

He hopes that your Assembly will be able to see that a stream of itinerant teachers and pioneers constantly goes out to the weak centres in the new territories, to consolidate the Faith and establish new Assemblies, to teach and encourage people, and carry to them both the light and the love of Bahá'u'lláh.

(From a letter dated 4 July 1956 written on behalf of Shoghi Effendi to the National Spiritual Assembly of South and West Africa)

267. I feel confident that your Assembly, now standing on the threshold of a period of unparalleled expansion, will, through its high endeavours, lend a tremendous impetus to the historic process which has been set in motion in recent years, and will, through its achievements, attract the manifold blessings of Bahá'u'lláh.

The path you are now called upon to tread is long, steep and thorny. As the work in which you are engaged develops, and is steadily consolidated, individuals and institutions inimical to the Faith, and jealous of its rising prestige, will exert their utmost to undermine the foundations you are now laying and to extinguish the light which has been so brilliantly kindled by pioneers, settlers and newly enrolled believers throughout the territories now included within your jurisdiction.

(In the handwriting of Shoghi Effendi, appended to a letter dated 6 July 1956 written on behalf of Shoghi Effendi to the National Spiritual Assembly of Central and East Africa)

268. The question of your budget, which you have raised in your letter, is one of great importance. In spite of the numbers which you represent and the enthusiasm of the Bahá'ís, your Assembly must face the fact that it represents a very poor Community, financially. Any over-ambitious budget, which would place an oppressive financial burden on the friends, would be highly unwise, because, unless it is met, it will give them a feeling at the end of the year of intense frustration.

He thinks that what you have outlined is too much. Your Assembly will have to, particularly during this first year of its existence, be less ambitious as regards projects involving money, and devote itself particularly to encouraging the friends, reinforcing the foundations of the Local Assemblies, assisting the Groups to attain Assembly status, and deepening in every way it can the education of the African friends in the Faith. The other National Spiritual Assemblies, as you know, are having their own problems financially; and, although there is no objection to appealing to them to give you some help, the Guardian doubts very much whether they will be in a position to add very substantially to your funds at this time.

(From a letter dated 6 July 1956 written on behalf of Shoghi Effendi to the
National Spiritual Assembly of Central and East Africa)

269. The beloved Guardian was very happy to review the map, with you notations thereon, showing the number of Indian Bahá'ís. He feels this is a real victory for the Faith, as the Master has spoken so often of the strength of character and latent capacity of the original peoples of the American continent. Thus, the quickening of some of them is a historic turning-point in the activity of the Faith, as well as the life of these people.

(From a letter dated 31 July 1956 written on behalf of Shoghi Effendi to an
individual believer)

270. He feels the Persians can render the utmost assistance to the teaching work, wherever they settle; but they must go on the basis of pioneers, and take up residence where they can render the best service to the Cause of God. It does little good for the Faith to have large groups of Persians settled in a city, and thus constitute an Assembly. When they move the Assembly falls. What we need in all areas is native believers. The pioneers should be in the minority, and aid the natives to shoulder the responsibility of the Faith.

(From a letter dated 17 February 1957 written on behalf of Shoghi Effendi
to an individual believer)

271. ...to stimulate the process of the conversion of both the Negroes and the American Indians, and ensure their active participation in the administration of the affairs of Bahá'í communities...

(From a letter dated April 1957 written by Shoghi Effendi to the
Conventions of Argentina, Chile, Uruguay, Paraguay and Bolivia; of
Brazil, Peru, Colombia, Ecuador and Venezuela; of Central America and
Mexico; and of the Greater Antilles)

272. As you formulate your plans and carry them out for the work entrusted to you during the next six years, he wishes you to particularly bear in mind the need of teaching Maoris. These original discoverers of New Zealand are of a very fine race, and they are a people long admired for their noble qualities; and special effort should be made, not only to contract the Maoris in the cities, and draw them into the Faith, but to go to their towns and live amongst them and establish Assemblies in which at least the majority of the believers will be Maoris, if not all. This would be indeed a worthy achievement.

(From a letter dated 27 June 1957 written on behalf of Shoghi Effendi to the National Spiritual Assembly of New Zealand)

273.   He hopes there will be a great deal more teaching activity during the present year, and that the Latin American Bahá'ís will increasingly feel that this is their Faith, and consequently their obligation, primarily, to spread it amongst their own people. Great as are the services rendered by pioneers, and unforgettable as are the deeds they accomplish, they cannot take the place of the indigenous element, which must constitute the bedrock of the Community, carry on its own affairs, build its own institutions, support its own funds, publish its own literature etc. A mother gives birth to a child, but the child then has to grow for itself. The older it gets, the more responsible it is for its own acts. The Latin American friends are rapidly coming of age, and they are showing this by the manner in which they are arising to serve the Faith, to demonstrate it, to sacrifice for it, to protect it and consolidate it.

(From a letter dated 3 July 1957 written on behalf of Shoghi Effendi to the National Spiritual Assembly of Brazil, Peru, Colombia, Ecuador and Venezuela)

274.   As the situation in the world, and in your part of it, is steadily worsening no time can be lost by the friends in rising to higher levels of devotion and service, and particularly of spiritual awareness. It is our duty to redeem as many of our fellow-men as we possibly can, whose hearts are enlightened, before some great catastrophe overtakes them, in which they will either be hopelessly swallowed up or come out purified and strengthened, and ready to serve. The more believers there are to stand forth as beacons in the darkness whenever that time does come, the better; hence the supreme importance of the teaching work at this time.

As he has written the Central and East Africa Assembly, he feels that the friends should be very careful not to place hindrances in the way of those who wish to accept the Faith. If we make the requirements too rigorous, we will cool off the initial enthusiasm, rebuff the hearts and cease to expand rapidly. The essential thing is that the candidate for enrolment should believe in his heart in the truth of Bahá'u'lláh. Whether he is literate or illiterate, informed of all the Teachings or not, is beside the point entirely. When the spark of faith exists the essential Message is there, and gradually everything else can be added unto it. The process of educating people of different customs and backgrounds must be done with the greatest patience and understanding, and rules and regulations not imposed upon them, except where a rock-bottom essential is in question. He feels sure that your Assembly is capable of carrying on its work in this spirit, and of fanning the hearts to flame through the fire of the love of God, rather than putting out the first sparks with bucketsful of administrative information and regulations.

(From a letter dated 9 July 1957 written on behalf of Shoghi Effendi to the National Spiritual Assembly of South and West Africa)

275.   He feels that the goals you have set yourself for your Seven Year Plan are excellent. The most important work of all of course is to confirm as many new believers as possible, wherever and whoever they may be, with special attention given to the Africans, who are the very purpose of the pioneers' presence in that Continent.

(From a letter dated 14 July 1957 written on behalf of Shoghi Effendi to the National Spiritual Assembly of North West Africa)

276.   It is not enough to bring people into the Faith, one must educate them and deepen their love for it and their knowledge of its teachings, after they declare themselves. As the Bahá'ís are few in number, especially the active teachers, and there is a great deal of work to be done, the education of these new believers is often sadly neglected, and then results are seen such as the resignations you have had recently.

(From a letter dated 18 July 1957 written on behalf of Shoghi Effendi to the National Spiritual Assembly of Canada)

277.   The paramount task is, of course, the teaching work; at every session your Assembly should give it close attention, considering everything else of secondary importance. Not only must many new Assemblies be developed, as well as groups and isolated centres, but special attention must be focused on the work of converting the Indians to the Faith. The goal should be all-Indian Assemblies, so that these much exploited and suppressed original inhabitants of the land may realize that they are equals, and partners in the affairs of the Cause of God, and that Bahá'u'lláh is the Manifestation of God for them.

(From a letter dated 28 July 1957 written on behalf of Shoghi Effendi to the National Spiritual Assembly of Central America and Mexico)

278. The all-important enterprise, aimed at winning the whole-hearted allegiance of the members of various tribes of American Indians to the Cause of Bahá'u'lláh, and at ensuring their active and sustained participation in the conduct of its administrative affairs, must likewise be seriously considered and strenuously pursued.

(In the handwriting of Shoghi Effendi, appended to a letter dated 28 July 1957 written on behalf of Shoghi Effendi to the National Spiritual Assembly of Central America and Mexico)

279. As you formulate the goals which must receive your undivided attention during the coming years he urges you to bear in mind the most important one of all, namely the multiplication of the Spiritual Assemblies, the groups and the isolated centres; this will ensure both breadth and depth in the foundations you are laying for the future independent National Bodies. The believers should be urged to consider individually the needs in their immediate region, and to go forth to pioneer in near and distant cities and towns. They must be encouraged by your Assembly to remember that small people, often poor and obscure people, have changed the course of human destiny more than people who started out with wealth, fame and security. It was the Sifter of Wheat who, in the early days of our Faith, arose and became a hero and martyr, not the learned priests of his city!

...

He was particularly happy to see that some of the Indian believers were present at the Convention. He attaches the greatest importance to teaching the original inhabitants of the Americas the Faith. 'Abdu'l-Bahá Himself has stated how great are their potentialities, and it is their right, and the duty of the non-Indian Bahá'ís, to see that they receive the Message of God for this day. One of the most worthy objectives of your Assembly must be the establishment of all-Indian Spiritual Assemblies. Other minorities should likewise be especially sought out and taught. The friends should bear in mind that in our Faith, unlike every other society, the minority, to compensate for what might be treated as an inferior status, receives special attention, love and consideration.

(From a letter dated 29 July 1957 written on behalf of Shoghi Effendi to the National Spiritual Assembly of Argentina, Chile, Uruguay, Paraguay and Bolivia)

280.   He feels that those responsible for accepting new believers should consider that the most important and fundamental qualification for acceptance is the recognition of the station of Bahá'u'lláh in this day on the part of the applicant. We cannot expect people who are illiterate (which is no reflection on their mental abilities or capacities) to have studied the Teachings, especially when so little literature is available in their own language in the first place, and grasp all their ramifications, the way an African, say in London, is expected to. The spirit of the person is the important thing, the recognition of Bahá'u'lláh and His position in the world in this day. The friends therefore must not be too strict, or they will find that the great wave of loving enthusiasm with which the African people have turned to the Faith, many of them already accepting it, cools off; and being very sensitive, they will feel in some subtle way that they are rebuffed, and the work will suffer.

The purpose of the new National Assemblies in Africa, and the purpose of any administrative body, is to carry the Message to the people and enlist the sincere under the banner of this Faith.

Your Assembly must never lose sight of this for a moment, and must go on courageously expanding the membership of the communities under your jurisdiction, and gradually educating the friends in both the Teachings and the Administration. Nothing could be more tragic than if the establishment of these great administrative bodies should stifle or bog down the teaching work. The early believers in both the east and the west, we must always remember, knew practically nothing compared to what the average Bahá'í knows about his Faith nowadays, yet they were the ones who shed their blood, the ones who arose and said: "I believe", requiring no proof, and often never having read a single work of the Teachings. Therefore, those responsible for accepting new enrolments must just be sure of one thing - that the heart of the applicant has been touched with the spirit of the Faith. Everything else can be built on this foundation gradually.

He hopes that during the coming year it will be increasingly possible for the African Bahá'í teachers to circulate amongst the newly-enrolled Bahá'ís and deepen their knowledge and understanding of the Teachings.

...

First and foremost, the vital process of the conversion of the Africans must acquire a momentum which will surpass any hitherto witnessed in African Bahá'í history. Any barrier impeding the discharge of this pre-eminent duty must be determinedly swept aside. Simultaneously, the emergence of new centres, the conversion of groups into Assemblies and the multiplication of the Assemblies themselves, must be accelerated to an unprecedented extent. Nor must the pressing obligation to consolidate the firmly grounded local institutions of the Faith through their incorporation be, for a moment, neglected. The historic work, so laboriously initiated in the newly opened territories, and particularly in those where the Faith has not yet driven deep its roots, must, likewise, be rapidly and systematically reinforced. The establishment of Bahá'í endowments, the founding of local Hazíratu'l-Quds, the translation and dissemination of Bahá'í literature, must, moreover, receive the close and continued attention of the individual believers and particularly, their elected representatives. The institution of the National Fund, so vital and essential for the uninterrupted progress of these activities must, in particular, be assured of the whole-hearted, the every-increasing and universal support of the mass of believers, for whose welfare, and in whose name, these beneficent activities have been initiated and have been conducted. All, no matter how modest their resources, must participate. Upon the degree of self-sacrifice involved in these individual contributions will directly depend the efficacy and the spiritual influence which these nascent administrative institutions, called into being through the power of Bahá'u'lláh, and by virtue of the Design conceived by the Centre of His Covenant, will exert. A sustained and strenuous effort must henceforth be made by the rank and file of the avowed upholders of the Faith, whose number far surpasses that of their brethren residing in the areas administered by the three other Regional Spiritual Assemblies, to enable the communities under your jurisdiction to become self-supporting and ensure a steady flow of funds to the Treasury which now stands in dire need of substantial financial support.

(From a letter dated 8 August 1957 written on behalf of Shoghi Effendi to the National Spiritual Assembly of Central and East Africa)

281.   The Master has likened the Indians in your countries to the early Arabian Nomads at the time of the appearance of Muḥammad. Within a short period of time they became the outstanding examples of education, of culture and of civilization for the entire world. The Master feels that similar wonders will occur today if the Indians are properly taught and if the power of the Spirit properly enters into their living.

(From a letter dated 22 August 1957 written on behalf of Shoghi Effendi to the National Spiritual Assembly of Central America and Mexico)

282.   He was very happy indeed to learn of the very active manner in which the Canadian Bahá'ís have taken hold of this most important subject of teaching the Indians.

He attaches the greatest importance to this matter as the Master has spoken of the latent strength of character of these people and feels that when the Spirit of the Faith has a chance to work in their midst, it will produce remarkable results.

(From a letter dated 19 October 1957 written on behalf of Shoghi Effendi to the National Spiritual Assembly of Canada)

PROCLAIMING THE FAITH THROUGH MASS MEDIA

A Compilation Prepared by the Research Department of the Universal
House of Justice
June 1992

PROCLAIMING THE FAITH THROUGH MASS MEDIA

Extracts from the Writings of Bahá'u'lláh

283.   In this Day the secrets of the earth are laid bare before the eyes of men. The pages of swiftly-appearing newspapers are indeed the mirror of the world. They reflect the deeds and the pursuits of divers peoples and kindreds. They both reflect them and make them known. They are a mirror endowed with hearing, sight and speech. This is an amazing and potent phenomenon. However, it behoveth the writers thereof to be purged from the promptings of evil passions and desires and to be attired with the raiment of justice and equity. They should enquire into situations as much as possible and ascertain the facts, then set them down in writing.

("Tablets of Bahá'u'lláh Revealed after the Kitáb-i-Aqdas" (Wilmette:
Bahá'í Publishing Trust, 1988), p. 39)

284.   O newspapers published throughout the cities and countries of the world! Have ye heard the groan of the downtrodden, and have their cries of anguish reached your ears? Or have these remained concealed? It is hoped that ye will investigate the truth of what hath occurred and vindicate it.

(From a Tablet translated from the Arabic)

285.   Say: O men! This is a matchless Day. Matchless must, likewise, be the tongue that celebrateth the praise of the Desire of all nations, and matchless the deed that aspireth to be acceptable in His sight. The whole human race hath longed for this Day, that perchance it may fulfil that which well beseemeth its station, and is worthy of its destiny. Blessed is the man whom the affairs of the world have failed to deter from recognizing Him Who is the Lord of all things.

("Gleanings from the Writings of Bahá'u'lláh" (Wilmette: Bahá'í
Publishing Trust, 1983), p. 39)

286.   Teach thou the Cause of God with an utterance which will cause the bushes to be enkindled, and the call "Verily, there is no God but Me, the Almighty, the Unconstrained" to be raised therefrom. Say: Human utterance is an essence which aspireth to exert its influence and needeth moderation. As to its influence, this is conditional upon refinement which in turn is dependent upon hearts which are detached and pure. As to its moderation this hath to be combined with tact and wisdom as prescribed in the Holy Scriptures and Tablets. Meditate upon that which hath streamed forth from the heaven of the Will of thy Lord, He Who is the Source of all grace, that thou mayest grasp the intended meaning which is enshrined in the sacred depths of the Holy Writings.

("Tablets of Bahá'u'lláh Revealed after the Kitáb-i-Aqdas", p. 143)

287.　　Thou hast written that one of the friends hath composed a treatise. This was mentioned in the Holy Presence, and this is what was revealed in response: Great care should be exercised that whatever is written in these days doth not cause dissension, and invite the objection of the people. Whatever the friends of the one true God say in these days is listened to by the people of the world. It hath been revealed in the Lawḥ-i-Ḥikmat: "The unbelievers have inclined their ears towards us in order to hear that which might enable them to cavil against God, the Help in Peril, the Self-Subsisting."[1] Whatever is written should not transgress the bounds of tact and wisdom, and in the words used there should lie hid the property of milk, so that the children of the world may be nurtured therewith, and attain maturity. We have said in the past that one word hath the influence of spring and causeth hearts to become fresh and verdant, while another is like unto blight which causeth the blossoms and flowers to wither. God grant that authors among the friends will write in such a way as would be acceptable to fair-minded souls, and not lead to cavilling by the people.

(From a Tablet translated from the Persian and Arabic)

Extract from the Writings of 'Abdu'l-Bahá

288.　　It is therefore urgent that beneficial articles and books be written, clearly and definitely establishing what the present-day requirements of the people are, and what will conduce to the happiness and advancement of society. These should be published and spread throughout the nation, so that at least

1　　Tablets of Bahá'u'lláh, p. 141

the leaders among the people should become, to some degree, awakened, and arise to exert themselves along those lines which will lead to their abiding honour. The publication of high thoughts is the dynamic power in the arteries of life; it is the very soul of the world. Thoughts are a boundless sea, and the effects and varying conditions of existence are as the separate forms and individual limits of the waves; not until the sea boils up will the waves rise and scatter their pearls of knowledge on the shore of life.

Thou, Brother, are thy thought alone,
The rest is only thew and bone.[2]

("The Secret of Divine Civilization" (Wilmette: Bahá'í Publishing Trust, 1983), pp. 109-110)

From Letters written on behalf of the Guardian to individual believers unless otherwise cited

289.   It is undoubtedly very important to have first-class articles, faithfully presenting the teachings of the Cause, appear in the outstanding papers. People that, for some reason or other, keep away from the Bahá'í gatherings, and who are nevertheless interested in the spirit and teachings they expound, might find their opportunity in reading such articles that appear in the papers.

If in every centre the friends could win the co-operation of at least one of the local papers, they could thereby start a teaching campaign far more effective than anything yet attempted.

(11 January 1932)

290.   Concerning the publication of Shoghi Effendi's general letter to the Western friends regarding the world order of Bahá'u'lláh in the local papers: Shoghi Effendi would willingly permit you to do it, either in part or as a whole. He hopes that it will arouse some interest in the Cause and stimulate the teaching work.

(17 May 1932)

---

2   Rúmí, The Mathnaví, II 2:277

291.   In regard to your wish of broadcasting the Message, Shoghi Effendi would advise you to consult with the Spiritual Assembly as to whether such an action meets their approval, and if so to ask their assistance and help for finding the best means through which to carry out your plan. The idea of a wireless station is rather ambitious and requires much financial expenditure. If, however, you find it feasible and within your financial capacity you should not hesitate to do so, inasmuch as this will enable you to spread the Cause in a much easier and more efficient manner.

(13 August 1933)

292.   He is fully alive to the difficulties facing the friends at the present time. But he would urge each and all to work harder than ever, and to persevere in order that the Faith may be better appreciated and understood by the public.

(11 February 1934 to a National Spiritual Assembly)

293.   In connection with your publicity releases, the Guardian wishes your Committee to lay particular emphasis on the fact that the Revelation of Bahá'u'lláh marks the coming of age of mankind, and that the principle of the oneness of humanity - which is the core and the distinguishing feature of His Message - is but an evidence of the fact that the world has attained the stage of maturity, and can, therefore, carry this principle of oneness into the concrete realm of social reality. The close relationship that exists between the Faith, the maturity of the world, and the Bahá'í teaching of the oneness of mankind should be carefully analysed and presented, so as to bring into relief the full significance of the Cause.

(5 February 1938 to a National Spiritual Assembly)

294.   The Cause, with all its power and perfection, is to a certain extent dependent on the people who compose its ranks, and no doubt in the future, as people possessing greater specialized abilities and talents join it, we shall see a marked advance in the methods it uses to propagate itself.

(14 October 1942)

295.   In connection with the radio work he has no specific suggestions to make, as he feels that those actively connected with it in the States know the possibilities better. However, he would suggest that the main consideration is to bring to the attention of the public the fact that the Faith exists, and its teachings. Every kind of broadcast, whether of passages from the Writings, or on topical subjects, or lectures, should be used. The people need to hear the word "Bahá'í" so that they can, if receptive, respond and seek the Cause out. The primary duty of the friends everywhere in the world is to let the people know such a Revelation is in existence; their next duty is to teach it.

(24 July 1943)

296.   He feels it would be excellent if the Cause could be introduced more to the people through the medium of radio, as it reaches the masses, especially those who do not take an interest in lectures or attend any type of meeting.

(7 March 1945)

297.   The matter of obtaining free time on the radio is one which the Radio Committee and the National Spiritual Assembly must decide upon: but the principle is that every effort should be made to present the teachings over the air as often as possible as long as the manner in which it is done is compatible with the dignity of our beloved Faith.

(15 August 1945)

298.   He was also very pleased to see that the Cause is receiving newspaper publicity there, and that you are winning the sympathetic interest of editors and people of importance. The Faith needs friends as well as adherents, and you should always endeavour to attract the hearts of enlightened leaders to its teachings.

(5 October 1945 to a Local Spiritual Assembly)

299.   He was very pleased to see the excellent publicity the Cause received in the Chicago Sunday "Tribune", and hopes more will be forthcoming, of a similar nature, all over the country. In this connection, he sees no objection to using the advice and services of non-Bahá'í experts, or agencies, as long as the purity of the teachings and the dignity of the Faith are maintained.

...

Likewise large, well-publicized meetings and interesting radio programmes should be concentrated on. Every effort should also be made to obtain wide, first-class publicity for the Faith in newspapers and magazines.

(21 December 1945 to a National Spiritual Assembly)

300.   So very much depends on how the Cause is presented to the public, and the Guardian is always anxious to see the friends devise new ways and means of teaching and publicity.

(25 February 1946)

301.   He still feels that the type of films you wish to produce for teaching the public and stimulating the Bahá'ís themselves, are of great importance, and he urges you not to give up this work which you are fitted to do, but rather to write again to the new National Spiritual Assembly and ask them to appoint a committee which will be able to really assist you.

The Bahá'ís should not always be the last to take up new and obviously excellent methods, but rather the first, as this agrees with the dynamic nature of the Faith, which is not only progressive, but holds within itself the seeds of an entirely new culture and civilization.

(5 May 1946)

302.   These slides of our Bahá'í Temple and various activities are very interesting, and open a new door on the teaching approach to the general public. The more interesting sets [that] can be collected and circulated amongst the friends the better...

(28 December 1946)

303.   Your suggestion for a motion picture about the Cause is very good in principle, but such a film would have to be of the highest order, and he feels you should turn to the National Spiritual Assembly for advice in this matter. As we cannot show the Founders of the Faith, out of respect for Their exalted station, a scenario about the Cause would have to be truly a masterpiece in order to have popular appeal.

(5 April 1947)

304.   He considers your radio contacts very important, and urges you to co-operate with the...National Assembly and in this way assist them and also follow administrative procedure - that is whenever direct Bahá'í broadcasts are envisaged.

(18 July 1947)

305. He approves of your desire to teach the principles of the Faith through radio. But he urges you to do all you can to always, however small the reference you are able to make to it may be, clearly identify or associate what you are giving out with Bahá'u'lláh. The time is too short now for us Bahá'ís to be able to first educate humanity and then tell it that the Source is this new World Faith. For their own spiritual protection people must hear of the name Bahá'í - then, if they turn blindly away, they cannot excuse themselves by saying they never even knew it existed! For dark days seem still ahead of the world, and outside of this Divine Refuge the people will not, we firmly believe, find inner conviction, peace and security. So they have a right to at least hear of the Cause as such!

(24 April 1949)

306. He feels that the projected radio broadcasts are of the utmost importance as they afford you an opportunity of bringing to many listeners a sense of the greatness of the Cause. In this connection he has some advice to give you: You should stick carefully to facts and beware of putting any interpretations of facts into it...The Guardian advises you not to introduce into a series for public consumption anything obscure or mystical...

(5 November 1949)

307. The friends must be very alert, vigilant, in giving information to the public: the enemies of the Faith, and readers such as the Ambassador, have access to the Press and might rightfully claim we have distorted facts not historically correct. We cannot be too careful and every statement made should be checked to ensure correct historical facts...

(22 January 1951 to a National Spiritual Assembly)

308. He was immensely pleased to hear of the presentation of the Faith over television, and considers that your Assembly has every right to feel proud of this achievement. It shows that when the strong desire to serve unites the members of a Bahá'í community, they literally break into new fields in their teaching efforts, and their reward is assured.

He hopes that you will succeed in pioneering in many new ways of bringing the Cause before the public; and he assures you all of his most loving prayers for the success of your work for the Faith.

(6 December 1951 to a Local Spiritual Assembly)

309.   The cable launching the World Crusade deals with some 26 different goals. In the two Press releases which you sent the Guardian, mention is made, and not too emphatically, of only a few of these goals. In asking that the Crusade be publicized, the Guardian had in mind a strong portrayal of what our goals are, publicizing all of them. No doubt, a strong public statement for the Press can be released by the National Assembly.

(5 December 1952 to a National Spiritual Assembly)

310.   The beloved Guardian has received the clippings from English newspapers and read them with keen interest; he attaches much importance to such publicity in journals of such high standing.

(30 August 1955 to a National Spiritual Assembly)

Extracts from Letters written by the Universal House of Justice

311.   It is essential that those responsible for Bahá'í public relations rid themselves of any concept of the Bahá'í community as merely one religious group among others. This is the Cause of God, struggling to spread His Message for today among a mankind that is receding farther and farther from Him.

(21 July 1968 to a National Spiritual Assembly)

312.   The proclamation of the Faith, following established plans and aiming to use on an increasing scale the facilities of mass communication must be vigorously pursued. It should be remembered that the purpose of proclamation is to make known to all mankind the fact and general aim of the new Revelation, while teaching programmes should be planned to confirm individuals from every stratum of society.

(Naw-Rúz 1974 to the Bahá'ís of the World)

313.   It is our hope that the great power of radio for proclamation, teaching and deepening may be mobilized wherever possible, and with the promising initiatives which have occurred in Ecuador and elsewhere we now anticipate the development of more widespread uses of the medium which will be of service to the Cause and to mankind.

(7 April 1974 to a National Spiritual Assembly)

Extracts from Letters written on behalf of the Universal House of Justice

314. Obviously, the principles of the Faith should not be paraphrased in public statements in such a way as to distort their meaning, but wisdom dictates how little or how much detail about a specific principle should be presented at any given time...

(18 June 1975 to a National Spiritual Assembly)

315. The main purpose at this time of any publicity related to the Bahá'ís of Iran is to take advantage of the fact that the press and other media are more than ever before ready to publish information about the Faith. Bahá'ís should seize this opportunity to proclaim the Faith, but not to attack the Government of Iran.

(8 April 1980 to a National Spiritual Assembly)

316. ...the main objective of the proclamation to the masses is not so much to deal with current, and often ephemeral, issues but to make known the fact of the new Revelation, the appearance of Bahá'u'lláh and all that event implies for the regeneration and guidance of the world. Of course, your announcement of the Great Message should be made in terms relevant to the people you are addressing and the problems which occupy their minds, but it is much more important to proclaim Bahá'u'lláh and His teachings rather than deal with the controversial issues of the day.

(19 October 1981 to a National Spiritual Assembly)

317. The great importance of mass media in the proclamation of the Faith is recognized by all, particularly at this time when the persecutions in Iran have opened many broadcasting doors.

The House of Justice appreciates the zeal of those who are developing this valuable programme plan for television production and distribution, and has observed the praiseworthy initiatives resulting in useful productions...

(16 May 1982 to a private corporation)

318. In response to your request for guidance on the best ways to approach artists in teaching the Faith, it can be said that in addition to those methods which attract people generally, artists will be responsive to art. When the sublime teachings of the Faith are reflected in artistic work, the hearts of people, including artists, will be touched. A quotation from the Sacred Writings or description of the art pieces as it relates to the Writings may provide the viewer with an understanding of the source of this spiritual attraction and lead him to further study of the Faith.

(21 July 1982 to an individual)

319.   Campaign for enlightenment of the Press: This is undoubtedly of great importance and is a field in which an agency such as...can be of great assistance. However,...[the agency] should not be left alone to explain Bahá'í materials to important editors; it would be much more effective for a knowledgeable Bahá'í representative with a suitable personality to participate in the press tour.

Media Training: This too is an excellent suggestion. When Bahá'ís are to appear on radio or television it is most important for the individual to be chosen with care and for that person to be given the necessary training so that a correct impression will be made on the hearers or viewers. A bad or clumsy presentation can produce a lasting bad effect and undo a great deal of earlier good work.

Information Material: Here the services of a non-Bahá'í agency can be vital. Like all groups, Bahá'ís tend to develop their own terminology which, while meaningful to Bahá'ís themselves, can be bewildering or even meaningless to a non-Bahá'í audience. The National Assembly or its appropriate committees will know, from the point of view of the Bahá'í teachings, what they want to say, but...[the agency] can help to cast this in a form in which it conveys the correct meaning to the public.

(20 March 1985 to a National Spiritual Assembly)

320.   Your letter...containing the news of your monthly television programmes was received by the Universal House of Justice with great pleasure.

This is a commendable achievement, and will afford your community every opportunity to become skilful in assembling and preparing suitable material for these regular transmissions. However, with regard to your question on the use of the Greatest Name in the videotaped introduction, we have been instructed to inform you that it is not appropriate to use the Greatest Name in this way. You may wish to choose another suitable symbol, perhaps

a nine-pointed star or some other design by which you may be recognized.
(4 August 1986 to a National Spiritual Assembly)

USE OF RADIO AND TELEVISION IN TEACHING

A Compilation Prepared by the Research Department of the Universal House of Justice

USE OF RADIO AND TELEVISION IN TEACHING

Extracts from letters written on behalf of Shoghi Effendi

321.   In regard to your wish of broadcasting the Message, Shoghi Effendi would advise you to consult with the Spiritual Assembly as to whether such an action meets their approval, and if so to ask their assistance and help for finding the best means through which to carry out your plan. The idea of a wireless station is rather ambitious and requires much financial expenditure. If, however, you find it feasible and within your financial capacity you should not hesitate to do so, in as much as this will enable you to spread the Cause in a much easier and more efficient manner.

(13 August 1933 to an individual believer)

322.   Your suggestion regarding the installation of a radio station in the Temple is truly splendid. But it remains to be seen whether the National Spiritual Assembly finds it financially feasible to undertake such a project, which is, beyond doubt, a very costly enterprise. Whatever the expenditure involved in this project, there is no reason why the believers should not start now considering seriously the possibility of such a plan, which, whe[n] carried out and perfected, can lend an unprecedented impetus to the expansion of the teaching work throughout America.

It is for the National Spiritual Assembly, however, to take the final decision in this matter, and to determine whether the national fund of the Cause is at present sufficiently strong to permit them to install a radio station in the Temple.

The Guardian feels, nevertheless, confident that this plan will receive the careful consideration of the National Spiritual Assembly members, and hopes that, if feasible, they will take some definite action in this matter.

(31 January 1937 to an individual believer)

323.   He read with interest the various suggestions you made to the National Spiritual Assembly, and feels they are fundamentally sound, especially the wider use of the radio. Unfortunately at the present time anything that would make a fresh demand on the financial resources of the Cause in America —

such as a Bahá'í-owned broadcasting station — is out of the question, as the friends are finding it difficult to meet the great needs of the teaching and Temple Funds. However the idea should, he feels, be kept in mind for future realization.

(14 October 1942 to an individual believer)

324. In connection with the radio work ... he would suggest that the main consideration is to bring to the attention of the public the fact that the Faith exists, and its teachings. Every kind of broadcast, whether of passages from the Writings, or on topical subjects, or lectures, should be used. The people need to hear the word "Bahá'í" so that they can, if receptive, respond and seek the Cause out. The primary duty of the friends everywhere in the world is to let the people know such a Revelation is in existence; their next duty is to teach it.

(24 July 1943 to an individual believer)

325. He feels it would be excellent if the Cause could be introduced more to the people through the medium of radio, as it reaches the masses, especially those who do not take an interest in lectures or attend any type of meeting.

(7 March 1945 to an individual believer)

326. The matter of obtaining free time on the radio is one which the Radio Committee and the National Spiritual Assembly must decide upon: but the principle is that every effort should be made to present the teachings over the air as often as possible as long as the manner in which it is done is compatible with the dignity of our beloved Faith.

(15 August 1945 to an individual believer)

327. He was sorry to learn through your cable that the project for a Bahá'í radio station can not be carried out at present; he considers that such a station would be a very great asset to the Cause, not only as a teaching medium and a wonderful form of publicity, but also as an enhancement of its prestige. He feels your Assembly should not drop the matter, but go on investigating ways to make such a project materialize as soon as possible.

(20 March 1946 to the National Spiritual Assembly of the United States and Canada)

328.   He hopes that a Bahá'í radio station will prove feasible during the coming years, as he considers it of great importance.
(4 May 1946 to the Radio Committee of the National Spiritual Assembly of the United States and Canada)

329.   The Bahá'ís should not always be the last to take up new and obviously excellent methods, but rather the first, as this agrees with the dynamic nature of the Faith which is not only progressive, but holds within itself the seeds of an entirely new culture and civilization.
(5 May 1946 to an individual believer)

330.   The Guardian approves in principle of a radio station, and sees no objection to its being in the Temple; but he considers the cost you quote too much of a burden at the present time for the Fund to bear, in view of the multiple expenses of the new Seven Year Plan. If there is any way it can be done for a price you feel the Fund could pay, and which would be more reasonable, he approves of your doing it. In any case the National Spiritual Assembly should strongly press for recognition as a Religious Body, and claim full rights to be represented on the air on an equal footing with other established Churches.
(20 July 1946 to the National Spiritual Assembly of the United States and Canada)

331.   He approves of your desire to teach the principles of the Faith through radio. But he urges you to do all you can to always, however small the reference you are able to make to it may be, clearly identify or associate what you are giving out with Bahá'u'lláh. The time is too short now for us Bahá'í's to be able to first educate humanity and then tell it that the Source is this new World Faith. For their own spiritual protection people must hear of the name Bahá'í — then, if they turn blindly away, they cannot excuse themselves by saying they never even knew it existed! For dark days seem still ahead of the world, and outside of this Divine Refuge the people will not, we firmly believe, find inner conviction, peace and security. So they have a right to at least hear of the Cause as such!
(24 April 1949 to an individual believer)

OPPOSITION

A Compilation Prepared by the Research Department of the Universal House of Justice

OPPOSITION

I. From the Writings of Bahá'u'lláh

332.   Behold how in this Dispensation the worthless and foolish have fondly imagined that by such instruments as massacre, plunder and banishment they can extinguish the Lamp which the Hand of Divine power hath lit, or eclipse the Day Star of everlasting splendour. How utterly unaware they seem to be of the truth that such adversity is the oil that feedeth the flame of this Lamp! Such is God's transforming power. He changeth whatsoever He willeth; He verily hath power over all things....

("Gleanings from the Writings of Bahá'u'lláh", rev. ed. (Wilmette: Bahá'í Publishing Trust, 1983), sec. 29, p. 72)

333.   Pay thou no heed to the humiliation to which the loved ones of God have in this Day been subjected. This humiliation is the pride and glory of all temporal honour and worldly elevation. What greater honour can be imagined than the honour conferred by the Tongue of the Ancient of Days when He calleth to remembrance His loved ones in His Most Great Prison? The day is approaching when the intervening clouds will have been completely dissipated, when the light of the words, "All honour belongeth unto God and unto them that love Him," will have appeared, as manifest as the sun, above the horizon of the Will of the Almighty.

...

Ere long the world and all that is therein shall be as a thing forgotten, and all honor shall belong to the loved ones of thy Lord, the All-Glorious, the Most Bountiful.

("Gleanings from the Writings of Bahá'u'lláh", sec. 140, pp. 305-6)

334.   Say: O people of God! Beware lest the powers of the earth alarm you, or the might of the nations weaken you, or the tumult of the people of discord deter you, or the exponents of earthly glory sadden you. Be ye as a mountain in the Cause of your Lord, the Almighty, the All-Glorious, the Unconstrained.

(Cited in Shoghi Effendi, "The Advent of Divine Justice" (Wilmette: Bahá'í Publishing Trust, 1984), p. 82)

335.   Say: Beware, O people of Bahá, lest the strong ones of the earth rob you of your strength, or they who rule the world fill you with fear. Put your trust in God, and commit your affairs to His keeping. He, verily, will, through the power of truth, render you victorious, and He, verily, is powerful to do what He willeth, and in His grasp are the reins of omnipotent might.

(Cited in Shoghi Effendi, "The Advent of Divine Justice" p. 82)

336.   It is incumbent upon all men, each according to his ability, to refute the arguments of those that have attacked the Faith of God. Thus hath it been decreed by Him Who is the All-Powerful, the Almighty. He that wisheth to promote the Cause of the one true God, let him promote it through his pen and tongue, rather than have recourse to sword or violence. We have, on a previous occasion, revealed this injunction, and We now confirm it, if ye be of them that comprehend. By the righteousness of Him Who, in this Day, crieth within the inmost heart of all created things: "God, there is none other God besides Me!" If any man were to arise to defend, in his writings, the Cause of God against its assailants, such a man, however inconsiderable his share, shall be so honoured in the world to come that the Concourse on high would envy his glory. No pen can depict the loftiness of his station, neither can any tongue describe its splendour. For whosoever standeth firm and steadfast in this holy, this glorious, and exalted Revelation, such power shall be given him as to enable him to face and withstand all that is in heaven and on earth. Of this God is Himself a witness.

("Gleanings from the Writings of Bahá'u'lláh", sec. 154, pp. 329-30)

337.   When the victory arriveth, every man shall profess himself as believer and shall hasten to the shelter of God's Faith. Happy are they who in the days of world-encompassing trials have stood fast in the Cause and refused to swerve from its truth.

("Gleanings from the Writings of Bahá'u'lláh", sec. 150, p. 319)

II. From the Writings of 'Abdu'l-Bahá:

338.   ...The darkness of error that has enveloped the East and West is, in this most great cycle, battling with the light of Divine Guidance. Its swords and its spears are very sharp and pointed; its army keenly bloodthirsty.

(Cited in Shoghi Effendi, "The Advent of Divine Justice", p. 6)

339. This day the powers of all the leaders of religion are directed towards the dispersion of the congregation of the All-Merciful, and the shattering of the Divine Edifice. The hosts of the world, whether material, cultural or political are from every side launching their assault, for the Cause is great, very great. Its greatness is, in this day, clear and manifest to men's eyes.

(Cited in Shoghi Effendi, "The Advent of Divine Justice", p. 6)

340. ...How great, how very great is the Cause! How very fierce the onslaught of all the peoples and kindreds of the earth. Ere long shall the clamor of the multitude throughout Africa, throughout America, the cry of the European and of the Turk, the groaning of India and China, be heard from far and near. One and all, they shall arise with all their power to resist His Cause. Then shall the knights of the Lord, assisted by His grace from on high, strengthened by faith, aided by the power of understanding, and reinforced by the legions of the Covenant, arise and make manifest the truth of the verse: "Behold the confusion that hath befallen the tribes of the defeated!"

(Cited in Shoghi Effendi, "The World Order of Bahá'u'lláh: Selected Letters", rev. ed. (Wilmette: Bahá'í Publishing Trust, 1982), p. 17)

341. The prestige of the Faith of God has immensely increased. Its greatness is now manifest. The day is approaching when it will have cast a tremendous tumult in men's hearts. Rejoice, therefore, O denizens of America, rejoice with exceeding gladness!

(Cited in Shoghi Effendi, "The World Order of Bahá'u'lláh: Selected Letters", p. 79)

342. O ye beloved of God! When the winds blow severely, rains fall fiercely, the lightning flashes, the thunder roars, the bolt descends and storms of trial become severe, grieve not; for after this storm, verily, the divine spring will arrive, the hills and fields will become verdant, the expanses of grain will joyfully wave, the earth will become covered with blossoms, the trees will be clothed with green garments and adorned with blossoms and fruits. Thus blessings become manifest in all countries. These favours are results of those storms and hurricanes.

...

Therefore, O ye beloved of God, be not grieved when people stand against you, persecute you, afflict and trouble you and say all manner of evil against you. The darkness will pass away and the light of the manifest signs will appear, the veil will be withdrawn and the Light of Reality will shine forth from the unseen [Kingdom] of El-Abhá. This we inform you before it occurs, so that when the hosts of people arise against you for my love, be not disturbed or troubled; nay rather, be firm as a mountain, for this persecution and reviling of the people upon you is a pre-ordained matter. Blessed is the soul who is firm in the path!

("Tablets of Abdul Baha Abbas", vol. 1 (Chicago: Bahá'í Publishing
Committee, 1930), pp. 12-14)

343.   ...a large multitude of people will arise against you, showing oppression, expressing contumely and derision, shunning your society, and heaping upon you ridicule. However, the Heavenly Father will illumine you to such an extent that, like unto the rays of the sun, you shall scatter the dark clouds of superstition, shine gloriously in the midst of Heaven and illumine the face of the earth. You must make firm the feet at the time when these trials transpire, and demonstrate forbearance and patience. You must withstand them with the utmost love and kindness; consider their oppression and persecution as the caprice of children, and do not give any importance to whatever they do. For at the end the illumination of the Kingdom will overwhelm the darkness of the world and the exaltation and grandeur of your station will become apparent and manifest...

(From a Tablet to an individual believer, published in "Bahá'í News" 10
(September 1910), pp. 1-2)

III. From the Writings of Shoghi Effendi:

344.   I am however assured and sustained by the conviction, never dimmed in my mind, that whatsoever comes to pass in the Cause of God, however disquieting in its immediate effects, is fraught with infinite Wisdom and tends ultimately to promote its interests in the world. Indeed, our experiences of the distant past, as well as of recent events, are too numerous and varied to permit of any misgiving or doubt as to the truth of this basic principle — a principle which throughout the vicissitudes of our sacred mission in this world we must never disregard or forget.

(From a letter dated 23 December 1922 to the National Spiritual Assembly
of the United States and Canada, published in "Bahá'í Administration:

Selected Messages 1922-1932" [rev. ed.], (Wilmette: Bahá'í Publishing Trust, 1980), p.27)

345.   That the Cause of God should in the days to come witness many a challenging hour and pass through critical stages in preparation for the glories of its promised ascendancy in the New World has been time and again undeniably affirmed by our departed Master, and is abundantly proved to us all by its heroic past and turbulent history....

(From a letter dated 23 February 1924 to the Bahá'ís of America, published in "Bahá'í Administration: Selected Messages 1922-1932", pp. 60-61)

346.   We cannot believe that as the Movement grows in strength, in authority and in influence, the perplexities and the sufferings it has had to contend with in the past will correspondingly decrease and vanish. Nay, as it grows from strength to strength, the fanatical defendants of the strongholds of Orthodoxy, whatever be their denomination, realizing the penetrating influence of this growing Faith, will arise and strain every nerve to extinguish its light and discredit its name. For has not our beloved 'Abdu'l-Bahá sent forth His glowing prophecy from behind the prison walls of the citadel of 'Akká — words so significant in their forecast of the coming world turmoil, yet so rich in their promise of eventual victory...

...

Dearly-beloved friends, upon us devolves the supreme obligation to stand by His side, to fight His battles and to win His victory. May we prove ourselves worthy of this trust.

(From a letter dated 12 February 1927 to the Bahá'ís of the West, published in "Bahá'í Administration: Selected Messages 1922-1932"), p. 123)

347.   Viewed in the light of past experience, the inevitable result of such futile attempts, however persistent and malicious they may be, is to contribute to a wider and deeper recognition by believers and unbelievers alike of the distinguishing features of the Faith proclaimed by Bahá'u'lláh. These challenging criticisms, whether or not dictated by malice, cannot but serve to galvanize the souls of its ardent supporters, and to consolidate the ranks of its faithful promoters. They will purge the Faith from those pernicious elements whose continued association with the believers tends to discredit the fair name of the Cause, and to tarnish the purity of its spirit. We should welcome, therefore, not only the open attacks which its avowed enemies persistently launch against it, but should also view as a blessing in disguise every storm of mischief with which they who apostatize their faith or claim to be its faithful exponents assail it from time to time. Instead of undermining the Faith, such assaults, both from within and from without, reinforce its foundations, and excite the intensity of its flame. Designed to becloud its radiance, they proclaim to all the world the exalted character of its precepts, the completeness of its unity, the uniqueness of its position, and the pervasiveness of its influence.

(From a letter dated 21 March 1930 to the Bahá'ís of the West, published in "The World Order of Bahá'u'lláh: Selected Letters", pp. 15-16)

348.   For let every earnest upholder of the Cause of Bahá'u'lláh realize that the storms which this struggling Faith of God must needs encounter, as the process of the disintegration of society advances, shall be fiercer than any which it has already experienced. Let him be aware that so soon as the full measure of the stupendous claim of the Faith of Bahá'u'lláh comes to be recognized by those time-honoured and powerful strongholds of orthodoxy, whose deliberate aim is to maintain their stranglehold over the thoughts and consciences of men, that this infant Faith will have to contend with enemies more powerful and more insidious than the cruellest torture-mongers and the most fanatical clerics who have afflicted it in the past. What foes may not in the course of the convulsions that shall seize a dying civilization be brought into existence, who will reinforce the indignities which have already been heaped upon it!

(From a letter dated 21 March 1930 to the Bahá'ís of the West, published in "The World Order of Bahá'u'lláh: Selected Letters", p. 17)

349.   We have only to refer to the warnings uttered by 'Abdu'l-Bahá in order to realize the extent and character of the forces that are destined to contest with God's holy Faith....

Stupendous as is the struggle which His words foreshadow, they also testify to the complete victory which the upholders of the Greatest Name are destined eventually to achieve. Peoples, nations, adherents of divers faiths, will jointly and successively arise to shatter its unity, to sap its force, and to degrade its holy name. They will assail not only the spirit which it inculcates, but the administration which is the channel, the instrument, the embodiment of that spirit. For as the authority with which Bahá'u'lláh has invested the future Bahá'í Commonwealth becomes more and more apparent, the fiercer shall be the challenge which from every quarter will be thrown at the verities it enshrines.

(From a letter dated 21 March 1930 to the Bahá'ís of the West, published in "The World Order of Bahá'u'lláh: Selected Letters", pp. 17-18)

350. Fierce as may seem the onslaught of the forces of darkness that may still afflict this Cause, desperate and prolonged as may be that struggle, severe as may be the disappointments it may still experience, the ascendancy it will eventually obtain will be such as no other Faith has ever in its history achieved....

Who knows but that triumphs, unsurpassed in splendour, are not in store for the mass of Bahá'u'lláh's toiling followers? Surely, we stand too near the colossal edifice His hand has reared to be able, at the present stage of the evolution of His Revelation, to claim to be able even to conceive the full measure of its promised glory. Its past history, stained by the blood of countless martyrs, may well inspire us with the thought that, whatever may yet befall this Cause, however formidable the forces that may still assail it, however numerous the reverses it will inevitably suffer, its onward march can never be stayed, and that it will continue to advance until the very last promise, enshrined within the words of Bahá'u'lláh, shall have been completely redeemed.

(From the Epilogue to "The Dawn-Breakers: Nabíl's Narrative of the Early Days of the Bahá'í Revelation", trans. and ed. Shoghi Effendi. (London: Bahá'í Publishing Trust, 1975), pp. 667-668)

351. The separation that has set in between the institutions of the Bahá'í Faith and the Islamic ecclesiastical organizations that oppose it — a movement that has originated in Egypt and is now spreading steadily throughout the Middle East, and will in time communicate its influence to the West — imposes upon every loyal upholder of the Cause the obligation of refraining from any word or action that might prejudice the position which our enemies have, in recent years and of their own accord, proclaimed and established.... Our adversaries in the East have initiated the struggle. Our future opponents in the West will, in their turn, arise and carry it a stage further. Ours is the duty, in anticipation of this inevitable contest, to uphold unequivocally and with undivided loyalty the integrity of our Faith and demonstrate the distinguishing features of its divinely appointed institutions.

(In the handwriting of Shoghi Effendi, appended to a letter dated 15 June 1935 written on his behalf to the National Spiritual Assembly of the United States and Canada, published in "Bahá'í News" 95 (October 1935), p. 2)

352. That the forces of irreligion, of a purely materialistic philosophy, of unconcealed paganism have been unloosed, are now spreading, and, by consolidating themselves, are beginning to invade some of the most powerful Christian institutions of the western world, no unbiased observer can fail to admit. That these institutions are becoming increasingly restive, that a few among them are already dimly aware of the pervasive influence of the Cause of Bahá'u'lláh, that they will, as their inherent strength deteriorates and their discipline relaxes, regard with deepening dismay the rise of His New World Order, and will gradually determine to assail it, that such an opposition will in turn accelerate their decline, few, if any, among those who are attentively watching the progress of His Faith would be inclined to question.

(From a letter dated 11 March 1936 to the Bahá'ís of the West, published in "The World Order of Bahá'u'lláh: Selected Letters", pp. 180-81)

353. Fierce and manifold will be the assaults with which governments, races, classes and religions, jealous of its rising prestige and fearful of its consolidating strength, will seek to silence its voice and sap its foundations. Unmoved by the relative obscurity that surrounds it at the present time, and undaunted by the forces that will be arrayed against it in the future, this community, I cannot but feel confident, will, no matter how afflictive the agonies of a travailing age, pursue its destiny, undeflected in its course, undimmed in its serenity, unyielding in its resolve, unshaken in its convictions.

(In the handwriting of Shoghi Effendi, appended to a letter dated 5 July 1938 written on his behalf to the National Spiritual Assembly of the United States and Canada, published in "Messages to America: Selected Letters and Cablegrams Addressed to the Bahá'ís of North America 1932-1946" (Wilmette: Bahá'í Publishing Committee, 1947) p. 14)

354.   The resistless march of the Faith of Bahá'u'lláh ... propelled by the stimulating influences which the unwisdom of its enemies and the force latent within itself both engender, resolves itself into a series of rhythmic pulsations, precipitated, on the one hand, through the explosive outbursts of its foes, and the vibrations of Divine Power, on the other, which speed it, with ever-increasing momentum, along that predestined course traced for it by the Hand of the Almighty.

(In the handwriting of Shoghi Effendi, appended to a letter dated 12 August 1941 written on his behalf to the National Spiritual Assembly of the United States and Canada, published in "Messages to America: Selected Letters and Cablegrams Addressed to the Bahá'ís of North America 1932-1946", p. 51)

355.   How can the beginnings of a world upheaval, unleashing forces that are so gravely deranging the social, the religious, the political, and the economic equilibrium of organized society, throwing into chaos and confusion political systems, racial doctrines, social conceptions, cultural standards, religious associations, and trade relationships — how can such agitations, on a scale so vast, so unprecedented, fail to produce any repercussions on the institutions of a Faith of such tender age whose teachings have a direct and vital bearing on each of these spheres of human life and conduct?

Little wonder, therefore, if they who are holding aloft the banner of so pervasive a Faith, so challenging a Cause, find themselves affected by the impact of these world-shaking forces. Little wonder if they find that in the midst of this whirlpool of contending passions their freedom has been curtailed, their tenets contemned, their institutions assaulted, their motives maligned, their authority jeopardized, their claim rejected.

(From a letter dated 25 December 1938 to the Bahá'ís of the United States and Canada, published in "The Advent of Divine Justice", pp. 2-3)

356.   Let not, however, the invincible army of Bahá'u'lláh, who in the West, and at one of its potential storm-centres is to fight, in His name and for His sake, one of its fiercest and most glorious battles, be afraid of any criticism that might be directed against it. Let it not be deterred by any condemnation with which the tongue of the slanderer may seek to debase its motives. Let it not recoil before the threatening advance of the forces of fanaticism, of orthodoxy, of corruption, and of prejudice that may be leagued against it. The voice of criticism is a voice that indirectly reinforces the proclamation of its Cause. Unpopularity but serves to throw into greater relief the contrast between it and its adversaries, while ostracism is itself the magnetic power that must eventually win over to its camp the most vociferous and inveterate amongst its foes....

(From a letter dated 25 December 1938 to the Bahá'ís of the United States and Canada, published in "The Advent of Divine Justice", p. 42)

357. We can discover a no less distinct gradation in the character of the opposition it has had to encounter — ... an opposition which, now, through the rise of a divinely appointed Order in the Christian West, and its initial impact on civil and ecclesiastical institutions, bids fair to include among its supporters established governments and systems associated with the most ancient, the most deeply entrenched sacerdotal hierarchies in Christendom. We can, at the same time, recognize, through the haze of an ever-widening hostility, the progress, painful yet persistent, of certain communities within its pale through the stages of obscurity, of proscription, of emancipation, and of recognition — stages that must needs culminate in the course of succeeding centuries, in the establishment of the Faith, and the founding, in the plenitude of its power and authority, of the world-embracing Bahá'í Commonwealth....

("God Passes By", rev. ed. (Wilmette: Bahá'í Publishing Trust, 1987), Foreword p. xvii)

358. Nor should a survey of the outstanding features of so blessed and fruitful a ministry omit mention of the prophecies which the unerring pen of the appointed Centre of Bahá'u'lláh's Covenant has recorded. These foreshadow the fierceness of the onslaught that the resistless march of the Faith must provoke in the West, in India and in the Far East when it meets the time-honoured sacerdotal orders of the Christian, the Buddhist and Hindu religions. They foreshadow the turmoil which its emancipation from the fetters of religious orthodoxy will cast in the American, the European, the Asiatic and African continents....

("God Passes By", p. 315)

359. Despite the blows leveled at its nascent strength, whether by the wielders of temporal and spiritual authority from without, or by black-hearted foes from within, the Faith of Bahá'u'lláh had, far from breaking or bending, gone from strength to strength, from victory to victory. Indeed its history, if read aright, may be said to resolve itself into a series of pulsations, of alternating crisis and triumphs, leading it ever nearer to its divinely appointed destiny....

("God Passes By", p. 409)

360.   The tribulations attending the progressive unfoldment of the Faith of Bahá'u'lláh have indeed been such as to exceed in gravity those from which the religions of the past have suffered. Unlike those religions, however, these tribulations have failed utterly to impair its unity, or to create, even temporarily, a breach in the ranks of its adherents. It has not only survived these ordeals, but has emerged, purified and inviolate, endowed with greater capacity to face and surmount any crisis which its resistless march may engender in the future.

("God Passes By", p. 410)

361.   Whatever may befall this infant Faith of God in future decades or in succeeding centuries, whatever the sorrows, dangers and tribulations which the next stage in its world-wide development may engender, from whatever quarter the assaults to be launched by its present or future adversaries may be unleashed against it, however great the reverses and setbacks it may suffer, we, who have been privileged to apprehend, to the degree our finite minds can fathom, the significance of these marvelous phenomena associated with its rise and establishment, can harbor no doubt that what it has already achieved in the first hundred years of its life provides sufficient guarantee that it will continue to forge ahead, capturing loftier heights, tearing down every obstacle, opening up new horizons and winning still mightier victories until its glorious mission, stretching into the dim ranges of time that lie ahead, is totally fulfilled.

("God Passes By", p. 412)

362.   No opportunity, in view of the necessity of ensuring the harmonious development of the Faith, should be ignored, which its potential enemies, whether ecclesiastical or otherwise, may offer, to set forth, in a restrained and unprovocative language, its aims and tenets, to defend its interests, to proclaim its universality, to assert the supernatural, the supranational and non-political character of its institutions, and its acceptance of the Divine origin of the Faiths which have preceded it....

(From a letter dated 5 June 1947 to the Bahá'ís of the West, published in "Citadel of Faith: Messages to America 1947-1957" (Wilmette: Bahá'í Publishing Trust, 1980), p. 23)

363. Indeed this fresh ordeal that has, in pursuance of the mysterious dispensations of Providence, afflicted the Faith at this unexpected hour, far from dealing a fatal blow to its institutions or existence, should be regarded as a blessing in disguise, not a "calamity" but a "providence" of God, not a devastating flood but a "gentle rain" on a "green pasture", a "wick" and "oil" unto the "lamp" of His Faith, a "nurture" for His Cause, "water for that which has been planted in the hearts of men", a "crown set on the head" of His Messenger for this Day.

(In the handwriting of Shoghi Effendi, appended to a letter dated 20 August 1955 written on his behalf to the National Spiritual Assembly of the United States, published in "Citadel of Faith: Messages to America 1947-1957", p. 139)

IV. From Letters Written on Behalf of Shoghi Effendi

364. ...when the very progress of the Cause on the one hand, and the corresponding decline in ecclesiastical organizations on the other will inevitably incite Christian ecclesiastical leaders to vehemently oppose and undermine the Faith, the believers will then have a real chance to defend and vindicate the Cause....

(From a letter dated 25 May 1938 to the National Spiritual Assembly of the United States and Canada)

365. The matter of refuting attacks and criticisms directed against the Cause through the press is, he feels, one which devolves on the National Spiritual Assembly to consider. This body, whether directly or through the agency of its committees, should decide as to the advisability of answering any such attacks, and also should carefully examine and pass upon any statements which the friends wish to send to the press to this effect. Only through such supervision and control of all Bahá'í press activities can the friends hope to avoid confusion and misunderstanding in their own minds and in the mind of the general public whom they can reach through the press.

The Guardian would advise, therefore, that henceforth you seek the guidance and approval of the National Spiritual Assembly in all your attempts to refute the criticisms of the enemies of the Cause, as there are certain cases when it is an absolute loss of time and energy, and even perhaps positively harmful, to counteract such attacks, which often lead to interminable and fruitless controversies. The National Spiritual Assembly can best advise you as to what action to take in such matters.

(From a letter dated 28 September 1938 to an individual believer)

366. The friends ... should not feel bewildered, for they have the assurance of Bahá'u'lláh that whatever the nature and character of the forces of opposition facing His Cause, its eventual triumph is indubitably certain.

(From a letter dated 30 August 1937 to an individual believer)

367. We have every reason to hope and believe that in the future many of the truly enlightened clergy may seek the shelter of Bahá'u'lláh, just as we feel certain that we may also expect at some future date a keen antagonism to our Faith on the part of those who do not see in it the salvation of the world, but rather challenge to their own fame and position.

(From a letter dated 6 July 1942 to a group of believers)

368. It seems both strange and pitiful that the Church and clergy should always, in every age, be the most bitter opponents of the very Truth they are continually admonishing their followers to be prepared to receive! They have become so violently attached to the form that the substance itself eludes them!

However, such denunciations as those your minister made publicly against you and the Bahá'í Faith can do no harm to the Cause at all; on the contrary they only serve to spread its name abroad and mark it as an independent religion.

(From a letter dated 7 February 1945 to an individual believer)

369. Although this may temporarily prove an embarrassment to your work, and a set-back, there is no doubt that it signalizes a step forward in the advance of the Faith; for we know that our beloved Faith must eventually clash with the entrenched orthodoxies of the past; and that this conflict cannot but lead to greater victories, and to ultimate emancipation, recognition and ascendancy.

(From a letter dated 8 April 1951 to two believers)

370. We are bound to meet with increasing opposition from Church-dominated countries, but our counter-moves must be carefully undertaken. He would like you to always consult him in matters which bring the Faith before government or Church bodies in cases of this kind.

(From a letter dated 23 November 1951 to the National Spiritual Assembly of the United States)

THE POWER OF DIVINE ASSISTANCE

A Compilation Prepared by the Research Department of the Universal
House of Justice
Revised August 1990

" It is the conviction of the House of Justice that the powers of heaven
and earth will, as repeatly asserted in the attached extracts,
mysteriously and unfailingly assist all those who will arise with love,
dedication, and trust in their hearts to teach the Cause, to promote
the Word of God, to deliver its healing message to receptive souls,
and to serve its vital interests."

THE POWER OF DIVINE ASSISTANCE

From the Writings of Bahá'u'lláh

371. Be not dismayed, O peoples of the world, when the day star of My beauty is set, and the heaven of My tabernacle is concealed from your eyes. Arise to further My Cause, and to exalt My Word amongst men. We are with you at all times, and shall strengthen you through the power of truth. We are truly almighty. Whoso hath recognized Me, will arise and serve Me with such determination that the powers of earth and heaven shall be unable to defeat his purpose.

("Gleanings from the Writings of Bahá'u'lláh", rev. ed. (Wilmette: Bahá'í Publishing Trust, 1984), sec. 71, p. 137; "A Synopsis and Codification of the Kitáb-i-Aqdas, the Most Holy Book of Bahá'u'lláh", 1st ed. (Haifa: Bahá'í World Centre, 1973), p. 14)

372. Let not your hearts be perturbed, O people, when the glory of My Presence is withdrawn, and the ocean of My utterance is stilled. In My presence amongst you there is a wisdom, and in My absence there is yet another, inscrutable to all but God, the Incomparable, the All-Knowing. Verily, We behold you from Our realm of glory, and shall aid whosoever will arise for the triumph of Our Cause with the hosts of the Concourse on high and a company of Our favoured angels.

("Gleanings from the Writings of Bahá'u'lláh", sec. 72, p. 139; "A Synopsis and Codification of the Kitáb-i-Aqdas, the Most Holy Book of Bahá'u'lláh", p. 16)

373. Dost thou believe thou hast the power to frustrate His Will, to hinder Him from executing His judgement, or to deter Him from exercising His sovereignty? Pretendest thou that aught in the heavens or in the earth can resist His Faith? No, by Him Who is the Eternal Truth! Nothing whatsoever in the whole of creation can thwart His Purpose....

Know thou, moreover, that He it is Who hath, by His own behest, created all that is in the heavens and all that is on the earth. How can, then, the thing that hath been created at His bidding prevail against Him?...

("Gleanings from the Writings of Bahá'u'lláh", sec. 113, p. 220)

374.   By the righteousness of God! Whoso openeth his lips in this Day and maketh mention of the name of his Lord, the hosts of Divine inspiration shall descend upon him from the heaven of My name, the All-Knowing, the All-Wise. On him shall also descend the Concourse on high, each bearing aloft a chalice of pure light. Thus hath it been foreordained in the realm of God's Revelation, by the behest of Him Who is the All-Glorious, the Most Powerful.

("Gleanings from the Writings of Bahá'u'lláh", sec. 129, p. 280)

375.   They that have forsaken their country for the purpose of teaching Our Cause — these shall the Faithful Spirit strengthen through its power. A company of Our chosen angels shall go forth with them, as bidden by Him Who is the Almighty, the All-Wise. How great the blessedness that awaiteth him that hath attained the honour of serving the Almighty!...

("Gleanings from the Writings of Bahá'u'lláh", sec. 157, p. 334)

376.   Great is the blessedness of him who hath in this Day cast away the things current amongst men and hath clung unto that which is ordained by God, the Lord of Names and the Fashioner of all created things, He Who is come from the heaven of eternity through the power of the Most Great Name, invested with so invincible an authority that all the powers of the earth are unable to withstand Him. Unto this beareth witness the Mother Book, calling from the Most Sublime Station.

("Tablets of Bahá'u'lláh Revealed after the Kitáb-i-Aqdas" [rev. ed.], (Haifa: Bahá'í World Centre, 1982), p. 48)

377.   This is the most great, the most joyful tidings imparted by the Pen of this Wronged One to mankind. Wherefore fear ye, O My well-beloved ones? Who is it that can dismay you? A touch of moisture sufficeth to dissolve the hardened clay out of which this perverse generation is moulded. The mere act of your gathering together is enough to scatter the forces of these vain and worthless people.

("Tablets of Bahá'u'lláh Revealed after the Kitáb-i-Aqdas", pp. 84-85)

378.   The source of courage and power is the promotion of the Word of God, and steadfastness in His Love.

("Tablets of Bahá'u'lláh Revealed after the Kitáb-i-Aqdas", p. 156)

379.   He, verily, will aid everyone that aideth Him, and will remember everyone that remembereth Him. To this beareth witness this Tablet that hath shed the splendour of the loving-kindness of your Lord, the All-Glorious, the All-Compelling....
(Cited in Shoghi Effendi, "The Advent of Divine Justice" (Wilmette: Bahá'í Publishing Trust, 1984), p. 76)

380.   Every single letter proceeding from Our mouth is endowed with such regenerative power as to enable it to bring into existence a new creation — a creation the magnitude of which is inscrutable to all save God. He verily hath knowledge of all things....
(Cited in Shoghi Effendi, "The Advent of Divine Justice", p. 80)

381.   It is in Our power, should We wish it, to enable a speck of floating dust to generate, in less than the twinkling of an eye, suns of infinite, of unimaginable splendour, to cause a dewdrop to develop into vast and numberless oceans, to infuse into every letter such a force as to empower it to unfold all the knowledge of past and future ages....
(Cited in Shoghi Effendi, "The Advent of Divine Justice", pp. 80-81)

382.   We are possessed of such power which, if brought to light, will transmute the most deadly of poisons into a panacea of unfailing efficacy.
(Cited in Shoghi Effendi, "The Advent of Divine Justice", p. 81)

383.   Say: Beware, O people of Bahá, lest the strong ones of the earth rob you of your strength, or they who rule the world fill you with fear. Put your trust in God, and commit your affairs to His keeping. He, verily, will, through the power of truth, render you victorious, and He, verily, is powerful to do what He willeth, and in His grasp are the reins of omnipotent might....
(Cited in Shoghi Effendi, "The Advent of Divine Justice", p. 82)

384.   By the righteousness of God, should a man, all alone, arise in the name of Bahá and put on the armour of His love, him will the Almighty cause to be victorious, though the forces of earth and heaven be arrayed against him....
(Cited in Shoghi Effendi, "The World Order of Bahá'u'lláh: Selected Letters", rev. ed. (Wilmette: Bahá'í Publishing Trust, 1982), p. 106)

385. By God besides Whom is none other God! Should any one arise for the triumph of our Cause, him will God render victorious though tens of thousands of enemies be leagued against him. And if his love for Me wax stronger, God will establish his ascendancy over all the powers of earth and heaven. Thus have We breathed the spirit of power into all regions.

(Cited in Shoghi Effendi, "The World Order of Bahá'u'lláh: Selected Letters", p.106)

From the Writings and Utterances of the Báb

386. Rid thou thyself of all attachments to aught except God, enrich thyself in God by dispensing with all else besides Him, and recite this prayer:

Say: God sufficeth all things above all things, and nothing in the heavens or in the earth or in whatever lieth between them but God, thy Lord, sufficeth. Verily, He is in Himself the Knower, the Sustainer, the Omnipotent.

Regard not the all-sufficing power of God as an idle fancy. It is that genuine faith which thou cherishest for the Manifestation of God in every Dispensation. It is such faith which sufficeth above all the things that exist on the earth, whereas no created thing on earth besides faith would suffice thee. If thou art not a believer, the Tree of divine Truth would condemn thee to extinction. If thou art a believer, thy faith shall be sufficient for thee above all things that exist on earth, even though thou possess nothing.

("Selections from the Writings of the Báb" [rev. ed.], (Haifa: Bahá'í World Centre, 1982), p. 123)

387. Say, verily any one follower of this Faith can, by the leave of God, prevail over all who dwell in heaven and earth and in whatever lieth between them; for indeed this is, beyond the shadow of a doubt, the one true Faith. Therefore fear ye not, neither be ye grieved.

Say, God hath, according to that which is revealed in the Book, taken upon Himself the task of ensuring the ascendancy of any one of the followers of the Truth, over and above one hundred other souls, and the supremacy of one hundred believers over one thousand non-believers and the domination of one thousand of the faithful over all the peoples and kindreds of the earth; inasmuch as God calleth into being whatsoever He willeth by virtue of His behest. Verily He is potent over all things.

Say, the power of God is in the hearts of those who believe in the unity of God and bear witness that no God is there but Him, while the hearts of them that associate partners with God are impotent, devoid of life on this earth, for assuredly they are dead.

("Selections from the Writings of the Báb", p. 153)

388. When the Day-Star of Bahá will shine resplendent above the horizon of eternity it is incumbent upon you to present yourselves before His Throne....
...

Ye have, one and all, been called into being to seek His presence and to attain that exalted and glorious station. Indeed, He will send down from the heaven of His mercy that which will benefit you, and whatever is graciously vouchsafed by Him shall enable you to dispense with all mankind.... Indeed if it be His Will He can assuredly bring about the resurrection of all created things through a word from Himself. He is, in truth, over and above all this, the All-Powerful, the Almighty, the Omnipotent.

("Selections from the Writings of the Báb", pp. 164-66)

389. Hallowed be the Lord in Whose hand is the source of dominion. He createth whatsoever He willeth by His Word of command 'Be', and it is. His hath been the power of authority heretofore and it shall remain His hereafter. He maketh victorious whomsoever He pleaseth, through the potency of His behest. He is in truth the Powerful, the Almighty. Unto Him pertaineth all glory and majesty in the kingdoms of Revelation and Creation and whatever lieth between them. Verily He is the Potent, the All-Glorious. From everlasting He hath been the Source of indomitable strength and shall remain so unto everlasting. He is indeed the Lord of might and power. All the kingdoms of heaven and earth and whatever is between them are God's, and His power is supreme over all things. All the treasures of earth and heaven and everything between them are His, and His protection extendeth over all things. He is the Creator of the heavens and the earth and whatever lieth between them and He truly is a witness over all things. He is the Lord of Reckoning for all that dwell in the heavens and on earth and whatever lieth between them, and truly God is swift to reckon. He setteth the measure assigned to all who are in the heavens and the earth and whatever is between them. Verily He is the Supreme Protector. He holdeth in His grasp the keys of heaven and earth and of everything between them. At His Own pleasure doth He bestow gifts, through the power of His command. Indeed His grace encompasseth all and He is the All-Knowing.

("Selections from the Writings of the Báb", p. 171)

390. Glorified art Thou, O God, Thou art the Creator of the heavens and the earth and that which lieth between them. Thou art the sovereign Lord, the Most Holy, the Almighty, the All-Wise. Magnified be Thy Name, O God, send down upon them who have believed in God and in His signs a mighty succour from Thy presence such as to enable them to prevail over the generality of mankind.

("Selections from the Writings of the Báb", p. 176)

391. Praised art Thou, O Lord! At Thy behest Thou dost render victorious whomsoever Thou willest, through the hosts of heaven and earth and whatsoever existeth between them. Thou art the Sovereign, the Eternal Truth, the Lord of invincible might.

("Selections from the Writings of the Báb", p. 177)

392. O Lord! Assist those who have renounced all else but Thee, and grant them a mighty victory. Send down upon them, O Lord, the concourse of the angels in heaven and earth and all that is between, to aid Thy servants, to succour and strengthen them, to enable them to achieve success, to sustain them, to invest them with glory, to confer upon them honour and exaltation, to enrich them and to make them triumphant with a wondrous triumph.

("Selections from the Writings of the Báb", p. 192)

393. Send forth, O God, such hosts as would render Thy faithful servants victorious. Thou dost fashion the created things through the power of Thy decree as Thou pleasest. Thou art in truth the Sovereign, the Creator, the All-Wise.

("Selections from the Writings of the Báb", p. 211)

394. Heed not your weaknesses and frailty; fix your gaze upon the invincible power of the Lord, your God, the Almighty. Has He not, in past days, caused Abraham, in spite of His seeming helplessness, to triumph over the forces of Nimrod? Has He not enabled Moses, whose staff was His only companion, to vanquish Pharaoh and his hosts? Has He not established the ascendancy of Jesus, poor and lowly as He was in the eyes of men, over the combined forces of the Jewish people? Has He not subjected the barbarous and militant tribes of Arabia to the holy and transforming discipline of Muḥammad, His Prophet? Arise in His name, put your trust wholly in Him, and be assured of ultimate victory.

(Addressed to the Letters of the Living, cited in "The Dawn-Breakers: Nabil's Narrative of the Early Days of the Bahá'í Revelation", trans. and ed. Shoghi Effendi (Wilmette: Bahá'í Publishing Trust, 1974), p. 94)

From the Writings and Utterances of 'Abdu'l-Bahá

395. These souls are the armies of God and the conquerors of the East and the West. Should one of them turn his face toward some direction and summon the people to the Kingdom of God, all the ideal forces and lordly confirmations will rush to his support and reinforcement. He will behold all the doors open and all the strong fortifications and impregnable castles razed to the ground. Singly and alone he will attack the armies of the world, defeat the right and left wings of the hosts of all the countries, break through the lines of the legions of all the nations and carry his attack to the very centre of the powers of the earth. This is the meaning of the Hosts of God.

("Tablets of the Divine Plan Revealed by 'Abdu'l-Bahá to the North American Bahá'ís", rev. ed. (Wilmette: Bahá'í Publishing Trust, 1980), pp. 47-48)

396. If in this day a soul shall act according to the precepts and the counsels of God, he will serve as a divine physician to mankind, and like the trump of Isráfil,[1] he will call the dead of this contingent world to life; for the confirmations of the Abhá Realm are never interrupted, and such a virtuous soul hath, to befriend him, the unfailing help of the Company on high. Thus

---

1   Believed to be the angel appointed to sound the trumpet on the Day of Resurrection to raise the dead at the bidding of the Lord.

shall a sorry gnat become an eagle in the fullness of his strength, and a feeble sparrow change to a royal falcon in the heights of ancient glory.

("Selections from the Writings of 'Abdu'l-Bahá" [rev. ed.], (Haifa: Bahá'í World Centre, 1982), sec. 8, p. 23)

397. Know thou of a certainty that thy Lord will come to thine aid with a company of the Concourse on high and hosts of the Abhá Kingdom. These will mount the attack, and will furiously assail the forces of the ignorant, the blind....

("Selections from the Writings of 'Abdu'l-Bahá", sec. 19, p. 43)

398. If a small number of people gather lovingly together, with absolute purity and sanctity, with their hearts free of the world, experiencing the emotions of the Kingdom and the powerful magnetic forces of the Divine, and being at one in their happy fellowship, that gathering will exert its influence over all the earth. The nature of that band of people, the words they speak, the deeds they do, will unleash the bestowals of Heaven, and provide a foretaste of eternal bliss. The hosts of the Company on high will defend them, and the angels of the Abhá Paradise, in continuous succession, will come down to their aid.

("Selections from the Writings of 'Abdu'l-Bahá", sec. 39, p. 81)

399. He will come to your aid with invisible hosts, and support you with armies of inspiration from the Concourse above; He will send unto you sweet perfumes from the highest Paradise, and waft over you the pure breathings that blow from the rose gardens of the Company on high. He will breathe into your hearts the spirit of life, cause you to enter the Ark of salvation, and reveal unto you His clear tokens and signs. Verily is this abounding grace. Verily is this the victory that none can deny.

("Selections from the Writings of 'Abdu'l-Bahá", sec. 157, pp. 186-87)

400. Rest ye assured that if a soul ariseth in the utmost perseverance and raiseth the Call of the Kingdom and resolutely promulgateth the Covenant, be he an insignificant ant he shall be enabled to drive away the formidable elephant from the arena, and if he be a feeble moth he shall cut to pieces the plumage of the rapacious vulture.

("Selections from the Writings of 'Abdu'l-Bahá", sec. 184, p. 209)

401.   The confirmations of Him Who is the Ever-Forgiving have wrapped every clime in light, the armies of the Company on high are rushing forward to do battle at the side of the friends of the Lord and carry the day...

("Selections from the Writings of 'Abdu'l-Bahá", sec. 193, p. 229)

402.   All praise and thanksgiving be unto the Blessed Beauty, for calling into action the armies of His Abhá Kingdom, and sending forth to us His never-interrupted aid, dependable as the rising stars....

("Selections from the Writings of 'Abdu'l-Bahá", sec. 195, p. 237)

403.   Whensoever holy souls, drawing on the powers of heaven, shall arise with such qualities of the spirit, and march in unison, rank on rank, every one of those souls will be even as one thousand, and the surging waves of that mighty ocean will be even as the battalions of the Concourse on high....

("Selections from the Writings of 'Abdu'l-Bahá", sec. 207, p. 260)

404.   It is clear that in this day, confirmations from the unseen world are encompassing all those who deliver the divine Message. Should the work of teaching lapse, these confirmations would be entirely cut off, since it is impossible for the loved ones of God to receive assistance unless they teach.

("Selections from the Writings of 'Abdu'l-Bahá", sec. 209, pp. 264-65)

405.   O ye servants of the Sacred Threshold! The triumphant hosts of the Celestial Concourse, arrayed and marshalled in the Realms above, stand ready and expectant to assist and assure victory to that valiant horseman who with confidence spurs on his charger into the arena of service. Well is it with that fearless warrior, who armed with the power of true Knowledge, hastens unto the field, disperses the armies of ignorance, and scatters the hosts of error, who holds aloft the Standard of Divine Guidance, and sounds the Clarion of Victory. By the righteousness of the Lord! He hath achieved a glorious triumph and obtained the true victory.

("Selections from the Writings of 'Abdu'l-Bahá", sec. 208, p. 264)

406.   Be not grieved at the smallness of your number and thank God for the power of your spirits. He shall assist you with such a confirmation whereat minds will be astonished and souls will be amazed.

("Tablets of Abdul Baha Abbas", vol. 1 (Chicago: Bahá'í Publishing

Committee 1930), p. 80)

407.   Be ye assured with the greatest assurance that, verily, God will help those who are firm in His Covenant in every matter, through His confirmation and favour, the lights of which will shine forth unto the east of the earth, as well as the west thereof. He will make them the signs of guidance among the creation and as shining and glittering stars from all horizons.

("Tablets of Abdul-Baha Abbas", vol. 1, p. 83)

408.   Arise with every power to assist the Covenant of God and serve in His vineyard. Be confident that a confirmation will be granted unto you and a success on His part is given unto you. Verily, He shall support you by the angels of His holiness and reinforce you with the breaths of the Spirit that ye may mount the Ark of Safety, set forth the evident signs, impart the spirit of life, declare the essence of His commands and precepts, guide the sheep who are straying from the fold in all directions, and give the blessings. Ye have to use every effort in your power and strive earnestly and wisely in this new century. By God, verily the Lord of Hosts is your support, the angels of heaven your assistance, the Holy Spirit your companion and the Centre of the Covenant your helper. Be not idle, but active and fear not....

("Tablets of Abdul-Baha Abbas", vol. 1, p. 162; "Bahá'í World Faith: Selected Writings of Bahá'u'lláh and 'Abdu'l-Bahá", [rev. ed.] (Wilmette: Bahá'í Publishing Trust, 1976), p. 362)

409.   By the Lord of the Kingdom! If one arise to promote the Word of God with a pure heart, overflowing with the love of God and severed from the world, the Lord of Hosts will assist him with such a power as will penetrate the core of the existent beings.

("Tablets of Abdul-Baha Abbas", vol. 2 (Chicago: Bahá'í Publishing Society, 1915) p. 348)

410.   Your Lord hath assuredly promised His servants who are firm and steadfast to render them victorious at all times, to exalt their word, propagate their power, diffuse their lights, strengthen their hearts, elevate their banners, assist their hosts, brighten their stars, increase the abundance of the showers of mercy upon them, and enable the brave lions (or teachers) to conquer.

    Hasten, hasten, O ye firm believers! Hasten, hasten, O ye steadfast!

Abandon the heedless, set aside every ignorant, take hold of the strong rope, be firm in this Great Cause, draw light from this Evident Light, be patient and be steadfast in this wise Religion! Ye shall see the hosts of inspiration descending successively from the Supreme World, the procession of attraction falling incessantly from the heights of heaven, the abundance of the Kingdom of El-ABHÁ outpouring continually and the teachings of God penetrating with the utmost power, while the heedless are indeed in evident loss.

("Tablets of Abdul-Baha Abbas", vol. 2, pp. 442-43)

411.   Today, any soul who looseneth his tongue in the delivery of Truth and is engaged in the diffusion of the fragrances of God, he shall undoubtedly be assisted and confirmed by the Holy Spirit and can resist the attacks of all the people of the world, [for the] power of the Realm of Might shall prevail. That is why thou seest that, although the disciples of Christ were physically weak and apparently vanquished by the persecution of every king, yet in the end were victorious over all and brought them under their protection.

("Tablets of Abdul-Baha Abbas", vol. 3 (Chicago: Bahá'í Publishing Society, 1916), p. 508)

412.   Should anyone in this day attach his heart to the Kingdom, release himself from all else save God and become attracted to the fragrances of holiness, the army of the Kingdom of ABHÁ will help him and the angels of the Supreme Concourse will assist him.

("Tablets of Abdul-Baha Abbas", vol. 3, p. 591)

413.   Remember not your own limitations; the help of God will come to you. Forget yourself. God's help will surely come!

When you call on the Mercy of God waiting to reinforce you, your strength will be tenfold.

Look at me: I am so feeble, yet I have had the strength given me to come amongst you: a poor servant of God, who has been enabled to give you this message! I shall not be with you long! One must never consider one's own feebleness, it is the strength of the Holy Spirit of Love, which gives the power to teach. The thought of our own weakness could only bring despair. We must look higher than all earthly thoughts; detach ourselves from every material idea; crave for the things of the spirit; fix our eyes on the everlasting bountiful

Mercy of the Almighty, who will fill our souls with the gladness of joyful service to His command 'Love One Another'.

("Paris Talks: Addresses given by 'Abdu'l-Bahá in Paris in 1911-1912",
10th ed. (London: Bahá'í Publishing Trust, 1979), pp. 38-39)

414.   How great, how very great is the Cause; how very fierce the onslaught of all the peoples and kindreds of the earth! Erelong shall the clamour of the multitude throughout Africa, throughout America, the cry of the European and of the Turk, the groaning of India and China be heard from far and near. One and all they shall arise with all their power to resist His Cause. Then shall the Knights of the Lord, assisted by grace from on high, strengthened by faith, aided by the power of understanding and reinforced by the legions of the Covenant, arise and make manifest the truth of the verse: 'Behold the confusion that hath befallen the tribes of the defeated!'[2]

(Cited in Shoghi Effendi, "Bahá'í Administration: Selected Messages
1922-1932" [rev. ed.], (Wilmette: Bahá'í Publishing Trust, 1980), p. 123)

415.   The Báb hath said: "Should a tiny ant desire, in this day, to be possessed of such power as to be able to unravel the abstrusest and most bewildering passages of the Qur'án, its wish will no doubt be fulfilled, inasmuch as the mystery of eternal might vibrates within the innermost being of all created things." If so helpless a creature can be endowed with so subtle a capacity, how much more efficacious must be the power released through the liberal effusions of the grace of Bahá'u'lláh!

(Cited in Shoghi Effendi, "The Advent of Divine Justice", p. 46)

416.   The Kingdom of God is possessed of limitless potency. Audacious must be the army of life if the confirming aid of that Kingdom is to be repeatedly vouchsafed unto it.... Vast is the arena, and the time ripe to spur on the charger within it. Now is the time to reveal the force of one's strength, the stoutness of one's heart and the might of one's soul.

(Cited in a letter dated 28 January 1939 to the National Spiritual Assembly
of the United States and Canada, published in Shoghi Effendi, "Messages

---

2   Qur'án 38:11

to America: Selected Letters and Cablegrams Addressed to the Bahá'ís of North America 1932-1946" (Wilmette: Bahá'í Publishing Committee, 1947), p. 17)

417.　And now you, if you act in accordance with the teachings of Bahá'u'lláh, may rest assured that you will be aided and confirmed. In all affairs which you undertake, you shall be rendered victorious, and all the inhabitants of the earth cannot withstand you. You are the conquerors, because the power of the Holy Spirit is your assistant. Above and over physical forces, phenomenal forces, the Holy Spirit itself shall aid you.

(Published in "Star of the West", vol. 8, no. 8 (1 August 1917), p. 103)

418.　Be ye valiant and fearless! Day by day add to your spiritual victories. Be ye not disturbed by the constant assaults of the enemies. Attack ye like unto the roaring lions. Have no thought of yourselves, for the invisible armies of the Kingdom are fighting on your side. Enter ye the battlefield with the Confirmations of the Holy Spirit. Know ye of a certainty that the powers of the Kingdom of Abhá are with you. The hosts of the heaven of Truth are with you. The cool breezes of the Paradise of Abhá are wafting over your heated brows. Not for a moment are ye alone. Not for a second are ye left to yourselves. The Beauty of Abhá is with you. The Glorious God is with you. The King of Kings is with you.

(Published in "Star of the West", vol. 13, no. 5 (August 1922), p. 113)

From Letters and Cables Written by Shoghi Effendi

419.　Difficult and delicate though be our task, the sustaining power of Bahá'u'lláh and of His Divine guidance will assuredly assist us if we follow steadfastly in His way, and strive to uphold the integrity of His laws. The light of His redeeming grace, which no earthly power can obscure, will if we persevere, illuminate our path, as we steer our course amid the snares and pitfalls of a troubled age, and will enable us to discharge our duties in a manner that would redound to the glory and the honour of His blessed Name.

(From a letter dated 21 March 1932 written by Shoghi Effendi to the Bahá'ís of the United States and Canada, published in "The World Order of Bahá'u'lláh: Selected Letters", p. 67)

420. "Peter," 'Abdu'l-Baha has testified, "according to the history of the Church, was also incapable of keeping count of the days of the week. Whenever he decided to go fishing, he would tie up his weekly food into seven parcels, and every day he would eat one of them, and when he had reached the seventh, he would know that the Sabbath had arrived, and thereupon would observe it." If the Son of Man was capable of infusing into apparently so crude and helpless an instrument such potency as to cause, in the words of Bahá'u'lláh, "the mysteries of wisdom and of utterance to flow out of his mouth," and to exalt him above the rest of His disciples, and render him fit to become His successor and the founder of His Church, how much more can the Father, Who is Bahá'u'lláh, empower the most puny and insignificant among His followers to achieve, for the execution of His purpose, such wonders as would dwarf the mightiest achievements of even the first apostle of Jesus Christ!

("The Advent of Divine Justice", p.46)

421. The field is indeed so immense, the period so critical, the Cause so great, the workers so few, the time so short, the privilege so priceless, that no follower of the Faith of Bahá'u'lláh, worthy to bear His name, can afford a moment's hesitation. That God-born Force, irresistible in its sweeping power, incalculable in its potency, unpredictable in its course, mysterious in its workings, and awe-inspiring in its manifestations — a Force which, as the Báb has written, "vibrates within the innermost being of all created things," and which, according to Bahá'u'lláh, has through its "vibrating influence," "upset the equilibrium of the world and revolutionized its ordered life" — such a Force, acting even as a two-edged sword, is, under our very eyes, sundering, on the one hand, the age-old ties which for centuries have held together the fabric of civilized society, and is unloosing, on the other, the bonds that still fetter the infant and as yet unemancipated Faith of Bahá'u'lláh.

("The Advent of Divine Justice", pp. 46-47)

422. There is no time to lose. There is no room left for vacillation. Multitudes hunger for the Bread of Life. The stage is set. The firm and irrevocable Promise is given. God's own Plan has been set in motion. It is gathering momentum with every passing day. The powers of heaven and earth mysteriously assist in its execution. Such an opportunity is irreplaceable. Let the doubter arise, and himself verify the truth of such assertions. To try, to persevere, is to ensure ultimate and complete victory.

(In the handwriting of Shoghi Effendi, appended to a letter dated 28 January 1939 written on his behalf to the National Spiritual Assembly of the United States and Canada, published in "Messages to America: Selected Letters and Cablegrams Addressed to the Bahá'ís of North America, 1932-1946" (Wilmette: Bahá'í Publishing Committee, 1947), p. 17)

423. Faced with such a challenge, a community that has scaled thus far such peaks of enduring achievement can neither falter nor recoil. Confident in its destiny, reliant on its God-given power, fortified by the consciousness of its past victories, galvanized into action at the sight of a slowly disrupting civilization, it will — I can have no doubt — continue to fulfil unflinchingly the immediate requirements of its task, assured that with every step it takes and with each stage it traverses, a fresh revelation of Divine light and strength will guide and propel it forward until it consummates, in the fullness of time and in the plenitude of its power, the Plan inseparably bound up with its shining destiny.

(In the handwriting of Shoghi Effendi, appended to a letter dated 4 July 1939 written on his behalf to the National Spiritual Assembly of the United States and Canada, published in "Messages to America: Selected Letters and Cablegrams Addressed to the Bahá'ís of North America, 1932-1946", p. 26)

424. The field, in all its vastness and fertility, is wide open and near at hand. The harvest is ripe. The hour is overdue. The signal has been given. The spiritual forces mysteriously released are already operating with increasing momentum, unchallenged and unchecked. Victory, speedy and unquestioned, is assured to whomsoever will arise and respond to this second, this urgent and vital call.

(In the handwriting of Shoghi Effendi, appended to a letter dated 28 July 1939 written on his behalf to the National Spiritual Assembly of the United States and Canada, published in "Messages to America: Selected Letters and Cablegrams Addressed to the Bahá'ís of North America, 1932-1946", pp. 28-29)

425. The vastness of the field, the smallness of your numbers, the indifference of the masses, must neither discourage nor appal you. You should at all times fix your gaze on the promise of Bahá'u'lláh, put your whole trust in His creative Word, recall the past and manifold evidences of His all-encompassing and resistless power, and arise to become worthy and exemplary recipients of His all-sustaining grace and blessings.

(In the handwriting of Shoghi Effendi, appended to a letter dated 29 June 1941 written on his behalf to the National Spiritual Assembly of India, published in "Dawn of a New Day" (New Delhi: Bahá'í Publishing Trust, n.d. [1970]), p. 90)

426.　If the friends, individually and collectively, play their part and exert their utmost the abundant blessings of Bahá'u'lláh will be fully vouchsafed, and the triumph of the Plan will mark a glorious chapter in the history of the Faith.

(In the handwriting of Shoghi Effendi, appended to a letter dated 18 December 1945 written on his behalf to the National Spiritual Assembly of the British Isles)

427.　...FORCES MYSTERIOUSLY RELEASED DESIGNED DIRECT OPERATION STIMULATE PROCESSES ENSURE CONSUMMATION SECOND STAGE DIVINE PLAN INCONCEIVABLY POTENT. FULL RAPID USE THESE FORCES BY ORGANIZED COMMUNITY ALIVE SUBLIMITY MISSION IMPERATIVE, MANIFOLD AGENCIES LOCAL REGIONAL NATIONAL INTERCONTINENTAL DIRECTLY RESPONSIBLE PROSECUTION PLAN NOW CALLED UPON ACHIEVE RESPECTIVE SPHERES ... SUCCESSES SO CONSPICUOUS AS SHALL IMMEASURABLY FORTIFY HOPES WINNING STIPULATED TIME TOTAL DECISIVE VICTORY....

(From a cable dated 6 October 1946 to the National Spiritual Assembly of the United States and Canada, published in "Messages to America: Selected Letters and Cablegrams Addressed to the Bahá'ís of North America 1932-1946", p. 108)

428.　The invisible hosts of the Kingdom are ready and eager to rush forth to the assistance of such as will have the courage to weigh the issues involved and to take the decision commensurate with these issues....

(In the handwriting of Shoghi Effendi, appended to a letter dated 6 September 1949 written on his behalf to the National Spiritual Assembly of

the British Isles)

429. Time is short. Opportunities, though multiplying with every passing hour, will not recur, some for yet another century, others never again. However severe the challenge, however multiple the tasks, however short the time, however sombre the world outlook, however limited the material resources of a hard-pressed adolescent community, the untapped sources of celestial strength from which it can draw are measureless in their potencies, and will unhesitatingly pour forth their energizing influences if the necesssary daily effort be made and the required sacrifices be willingly accepted.

(In the handwriting of Shoghi Effendi, appended to a letter dated 18 December 1945 written on his behalf to the National Spiritual Assembly of the United States, published in "Citadel of Faith: Messages to America 1947-1957" (Wilmette: Bahá'í Publishing Trust, 1980), p. 85)

430. The invisible battalions of the Concourse on high are mustered, in serried ranks, ready to rush their reinforcements to the aid of the vanguard of Bahá'u'lláh's crusaders in the hour of their greatest need...

(In the handwriting of Shoghi Effendi, appended to a letter dated 23 November 1951 written on his behalf to the National Spiritual Assembly of the United States, published in "Citadel of Faith: Messages to America 1947-1957", p. 105)

431. LORD HOSTS KING OF KINGS PLEDGED UNFAILING AID EVERY CRUSADER BATTLING HIS CAUSE. INVISIBLE BATTALIONS MUSTERED RANK UPON RANK READY POUR FORTH REINFORCEMENTS FROM ON HIGH.

(From a cable dated 8 October 1952 to the Bahá'ís of the West published in "Messages to the Bahá'í World 1950-1957" (Wilmette: Bahá'í Publishing Trust, 1971), p. 44)

432. Putting on the armour of His love, firmly buckling on the shield of His mighty Covenant, mounted on the steed of steadfastness, holding aloft the lance of the Word of the Lord of Hosts, and with unquestioning reliance on His promises as the best provision for their journey, let them set their faces towards those fields that still remain unexplored and direct their steps to those goals that are as yet unattained, assured that He Who has led them to achieve such triumphs, and to store up such prizes in His Kingdom, will continue to assist them in enriching their spiritual birthright to a degree that no finite mind can imagine or human heart perceive.

(From a letter dated April 1956 to all National Spiritual Assemblies, published in "Messages to the Bahá'í World 1950-1957", p. 102)

433.   Delicate and strenuous though the task may be, however arduous and prolonged the effort required, whatsoever the nature of the perils and pitfalls that beset the path of whoever arises to revive the fortunes of a Faith struggling against the rising forces of materialism, nationalism, secularism, racialism and ecclesiasticism, the all-conquering potency of the grace of God, vouchsafed through the Revelation of Bahá'u'lláh, will, undoubtedly, mysteriously and surprisingly, enable whosoever arises to champion His Cause to win complete and total victory.

(In the handwriting of Shoghi Effendi, appended to a letter dated 19 July 1956 written on his behalf to the National Spiritual Assembly of the United States, published in "Citadel of Faith: Messages to America 1947-1957", p. 149)

434.   ...the sustaining grace promised to all those who will arise, with single-mindedness, courage, dedication and high resolve, to aid in the attainment of these noble objectives, is of such potency that no earthly power can resist the ultimate fulfilment of so glorious a task, or even delay its eventual fruition.

(In the handwriting of Shoghi Effendi, appended to a letter dated 27 June 1957 written on his behalf to the National Spiritual Assembly of the Bahá'ís of New Zealand)

435.   The Concourse on High watches over them ready to vouchsafe its aid and confer its blessings on their valiant and concerted endeavours. The Author of the Divine Plan will, as promised by Him in His epoch-making Tablets, assist them to surmount whatever obstacles they may encounter in their path, and crown their historic enterprise with a resounding victory.

The Founder of their Faith Himself will not fail to reward them, in His own Kingdom, and in accordance with His wisdom and bounty, for their share in the furtherance of the interests of His world-encompassing Order, and to exalt them amidst the company of His immortal saints and heroes dwelling in the Abhá Kingdom.

(In the handwriting of Shoghi Effendi, appended to a letter dated 2 July 1957 written on his behalf to the National Spiritual Assembly of the Bahá'ís of the Iberian Peninsula)

From Letters Written on Behalf of Shoghi Effendi

436. Perhaps the reason why you have not accomplished so much in the field of teaching is the extent you looked upon your own weaknesses and inabilities to spread the message. Bahá'u'lláh and the Master have both urged us repeatedly to disregard our own handicaps and lay our whole reliance upon God. He will come to our help if we only arise and become an active channel for God's grace. Do you think it is the teachers who make converts and change human hearts? No, surely not. They are only pure souls who take the first step, and then let the spirit of Bahá'u'lláh move them and make use of them. If any one of them should even for a second consider his achievements as due to his own capacities, his work is ended and his fall starts. This is in fact the reason why so many competent souls have after wonderful services suddenly found themselves absolutely impotent and perhaps thrown aside by the Spirit of the Cause as useless souls. The criterion is the extent to which we are ready to have the will of God operate through us.

Stop being conscious of your frailties, therefore; have a perfect reliance upon God; let your heart burn with the desire to serve His mission and proclaim His call; and you will observe how eloquence and the power to change human hearts will come as a matter of course.

Shoghi Effendi will surely pray for your success if you should arise and start to teach. In fact the mere act of arising will win for you God's help and blessings.

(Dated 31 March 1932 to an individual believer)

437. You should never look at your own limitations, much less allow them to deter you from promoting the Message. For the believers, whether capable or not, whether poor or rich, and whether influential or obscure, are after all but mere channels through which God carries His message to mankind. They are instruments, whereby He communicates His will to His people. The friends, therefore, must cease looking at their own deficiencies in a way that would kill in them the spirit of initiative and of service. They should have confidence in the divine assistance promised to them by Bahá'u'lláh, and strengthened and revived by such an assurance they should continue to toil till the very end of their life.

(Dated 18 March 1934 to an individual believer)

438.   The invisible hosts of the Kingdom are ready to extend to you all the assistance you need, and through them you will no doubt succeed in removing every obstacle in your way, and in fulfilling this most cherished desire of your heart. Bahá'u'lláh has given us [a] promise that should we persevere in our efforts and repose all our confidence in Him the doors of success will be widely open before us....

(Dated 22 September 1936 to an individual believer)

439.   The harder you strive to attain your goal, the greater will be the confirmations of Bahá'u'lláh, and the more certain you can feel to attain success. Be cheerful, therefore, and exert yourself with full faith and confidence. For Bahá'u'lláh has promised His Divine assistance to everyone who arises with a pure and detached heart to spread His holy Word, even though he may be bereft of every human knowledge and capacity, and notwithstanding the forces of darkness and of opposition which may be arrayed against him. The goal is clear, the path safe and certain, and the assurances of Bahá'u'lláh as to the eventual success of our efforts quite emphatic. Let us keep firm, and whole-heartedly carry on the great work which He has entrusted into our hands.

(Dated 3 February 1937 to an individual believer)

440.   The Bahá'í teacher must be all confidence. Therein lies his strength and the secret of his success. Though single-handed, and no matter how great the apathy of the people around you may be, you should have faith that the hosts of the Kingdom are on your side, and that through their help you are bound to overcome the forces of darkness that are facing the Cause of God. Persevere, be happy and confident, therefore.

(Dated 30 June 1937 to an individual believer)

441.   ...he would advise you to persevere in the task you have set your heart to accomplish, confident that through Divine assistance you will be able, sooner or later, to attain your goal. Reliance on God is indeed the strongest and safest weapon which the Bahá'í teacher can carry. For by its means no earthly power can remain unconquered, and no obstacle become insuperable.

(Dated 27 March 1938 to an individual believer)

442. Smallness of numbers, lack of skilled teachers, and modesty of means should not discourage or deter them. They must remember the glorious history of the Cause, which, both East and West, was established by dedicated souls who, for the most part, were neither rich, famous, nor well educated, but whose devotion, zeal and self-sacrifice overcame every obstacle and won miraculous victories for the Faith of God.... Let them dedicate themselves — young and old, men and women alike — and go forth and settle in new districts, travel, and teach in spite of lack of experience, and be assured that Bahá'u'lláh has promised to aid all those who arise in His Name. His strength will sustain them; their own weakness is unimportant.

(Dated 29 June 1941 to the National Spiritual Assembly of the Bahá'ís of India, published in "Dawn of a New Day", p.89)

443. Bahá'u'lláh has said that God will assist all those who arise in His service. The more you labour for His Faith, the more He will aid and bless you.

(Dated 23 November 1941 to the Bahá'ís of Quito, Ecuador)

444. If the friends always waited until they were fully qualified to do any particular task, the work of the Cause would be almost at a standstill! But the very act of striving to serve, however unworthy one may feel, attracts the blessings of God and enables one to become more fitted for the task.

(Dated 4 May 1942 to an individual believer)

445. When once a few bold, self-sacrificing individuals have arisen to serve, their example will no doubt encourage other timid, would-be pioneers to follow in their footsteps. The history of our Faith is full of records of the remarkable things achieved by really very simple, insignificant individuals, who became veritable beacons and towers of strength through having placed their trust in God, having arisen to proclaim His Message....

(Dated 27 March 1945 to the National Spiritual Assembly of the British Isles)

446. Once the friends start out to win the goals set in their Plan, they will find the Divine confirmations sustaining them and hastening its consummation....

(Dated 9 August 1945 to the National Spiritual Assembly of the British Isles)

447.　It shows that wherever and whenever the friends arise to serve, the mysterious power latent in this Divine Cause rushes in to bless and reinforce their labours far beyond their fondest hopes.

(Dated 18 February 1947 to an individual believer)

448.　Each one of us, if we look into our failures, is sure to feel unworthy and despondent, and this feeling only frustrates our constructive efforts and wastes time. The thing for us to focus on is the glory of the Cause and the Power of Bahá'u'lláh which can make of a mere drop a surging sea!

(Dated 13 October 1947 to an individual believer)

449.　...when we put our trust in Him, Bahá'u'lláh solves our problems and opens the way.

(Dated 12 October 1949 to an individual believer)

450.　Just one mature soul, with spiritual understanding and a profound knowledge of the Faith, can set a whole country ablaze — so great is the power of the Cause to work through a pure and selfless channel.

(Dated 6 November 1949 to an individual believer)

451.　At all times we must look at the greatness of the Cause, and remember that Bahá'u'lláh will assist all who arise in His service. When we look at ourselves, we are sure to feel discouraged by our shortcomings and insignificance!

(Dated 12 December 1950 to an individual believer)

452.　Today, as never before, the magnet which attracts the blessings from on high is teaching the Faith of God. The Hosts of Heaven are poised between heaven and earth, just waiting, and patiently, for the Bahá'í to step forth, with pure devotion and consecration, to teach the Cause of God, so they may rush to his aid and assistance. It is the Guardian's prayer that the Friends may treble their efforts, as the time is short — alas, the workers too few. Let those who wish to achieve immortality step forth and raise the Divine Call. They will be astonished at the spiritual victories they will gain.

(Dated 28 March 1953 to an individual believer)

453.   The Hosts of the Supreme Concourse are in martial array, poised between Earth and Heaven ready to rush to the assistance of those who arise to teach the Faith. If one seeks the confirmation of the Holy Spirit, one can find it in rich abundance in the teaching field. The world is seeking as never before, and if the Friends will arise with new determination, fully consecrated to the noble task ahead of them, victory after victory will be won for the Glorious Faith of God.

(Dated 2 February 1956 to an individual believer)

454.   The Friends must realize the Power of the Holy Spirit which is manifest and quickening them at this time through the appearance of Bahá'u'lláh. There is no force of heaven or earth which can affect them if they place themselves wholly under the influence of the Holy Spirit and under its guidance....

(Dated 11 August 1957 to an individual believer)

Index

Note: All references are to extract numbers

T

Taiwan 44
teach(teaching) 22, 31, 32, 34, 35, 37, 38, 39, 40, 44, 45, 49, 51, 53, 60, 68, 79, 84, 88, 96, 110, 113, 114, 136, 145, 156, 164, 234, 260, 295, 301, 305
  aborigines 143
  artists 318
  attracts blessings 136
    leaders 193, 201
  avoid controversial issues 117
  choose one person 76, 79
  committees 167, 168, 170
  consolidation 23, 25, 29, 32, 35, 41, 45, 169
  constructively 114
  distinctive pamphlets 154
  diverse activities 31
  divine charter of 48
  effective 119, 140, 148, 153, 289
  efficient structure 25, 89
  essence of 75
  essential requisites of 81
  expansion 23, 25, 29, 45 (see also consolidation)
  firesides 126, 140
  food of spirit 40
  give with simplicity 166
  head cornerstone of service 134
  Home Front 148, 149
  Indians 247, 258, 277, 279, 282
  indigenous people 245
  individually 75, 120, 140, 157, 162
  institutes 168, 172, 258
  lapse in 404
  Maoris 272
  mass 41 (see also mass teaching)
  masses 23, 25